D1613069

OVS 384·545/
HEN

2 6 MAR 2004

Hertfordshire
COUNTY COUNCIL
Community Information

1 3 APR 2004

2 3 FEB 2005

2 6 MAR 2004

2 4 MAR 2007

Please renew or return items by the date shown on your receipt

www.hertsdirect.org/libraries

Renewals and enquiries: 0300 123 4049

Textphone for hearing or speech impaired users: 0300 123 4041

L32

L/C

PIRATE RADIO

THEN AND NOW

CENTRAL RESOURCES
LIBRARY

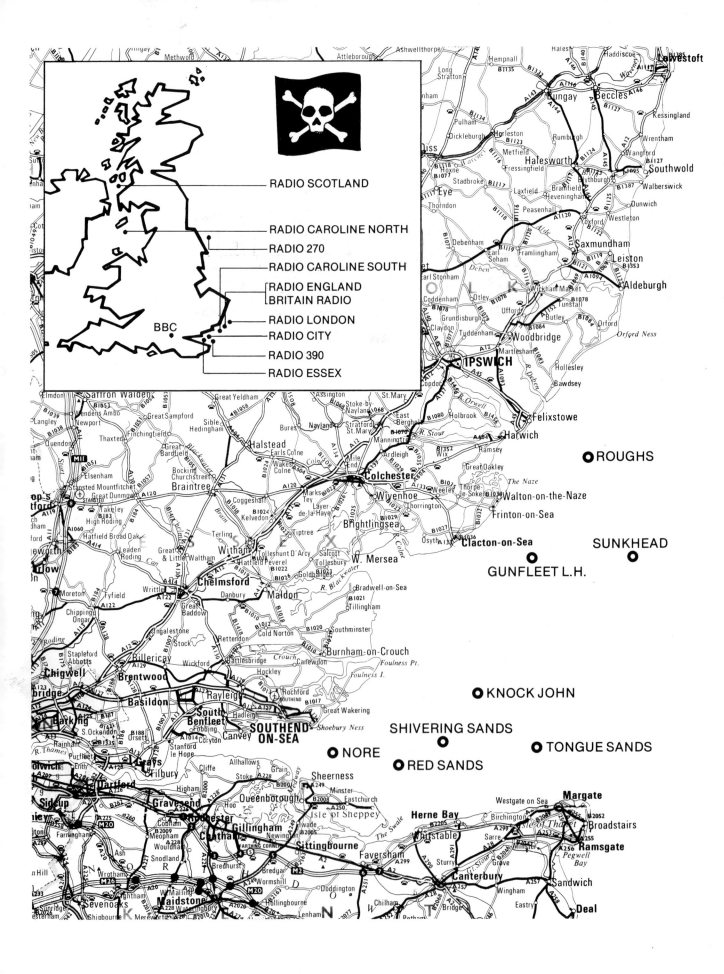

RADIO SCOTLAND

RADIO CAROLINE NORTH

RADIO 270

RADIO CAROLINE SOUTH

RADIO ENGLAND
BRITAIN RADIO

RADIO LONDON

RADIO CITY

RADIO 390

RADIO ESSEX

BBC

Stuart Henry & Mike von Joel

PIRATE RADIO

THEN AND NOW

BLANDFORD PRESS
POOLE • DORSET

First published in the U.K. in 1984 by Blandford Press,
Link House, West Street, Poole, Dorset BH15 1LL.

Distributed in the United States by
Sterling Publishing Co., Inc., 2 Park Avenue, New York, NY10016.

Copyright © 1984 Mike von Joel Stuart Henry

CENTRAL RESOURCES
LIBRARY

H31 232 2705

HERTFORDSHIRE
LIBRARY SERVICE

384.545

1863294

384.
545
HEN

British Library Cataloguing in Publication Data

Henry, Stuart
   Pirate radio.
   1. Pirate radio broadcasting
   I. Title   II. Von Joel, Mike
   384.54'53   HE8697.P57

ISBN 0 7137 1497 2

All rights reserved. No part of this book may be reproduced or transmitted
in any form or by any means, electronic or mechanical, including
photocopying, recording or any information storage or retrieval system,
without permission in writing from the Publisher.

Designed by Stuart Keen Mike von Joel
Conceived and Produced for Blandford Press
by Ziggurat Books, an imprint of AGP Newspapers Ltd.,
1/3 Garratt Lane, London SW18
Typeset by AGP Newspapers Ltd., London SW18
Printed in Great Britain by JB Offset Ltd.,
Marks Tey, Colchester.

3854

CONTENTS

Foreword 8/9
Acknowledgements 10
Introduction *by Bunny Lewis* 11
Events: 1958 — 1960 12-15
Tony Blackburn 16-21
Events: 1961 — 1963 22-25
Emperor Rosko 26-29
Dave Lee Travis 30-33
Events: 1964 34-39
Paul Burnett 40-45
Dave Cash 46-51
Events: 1965 52-55
Mark Wesley 56-63
Events: 1966 64-69
Johnnie Walker 70-75

Events: 1967 — 1968 76-79
Tony Prince Profile 80/81
Pete 'Boots' Bowman 82-87
Events: 1970 — 1972 88-91
Duncan Johnson 92-97
Events: 1973 — 1980 98-103
Stuart Henry 104
Kenny Everett 106-109
John Peel 110-113
Events: 1983 114-115
Events: 1984 116-117
Radio Jackie 118-120
Radio Nova 121-123
TUNE IN *Pirate Frequencies* 124-127
The Authors 128

Marine, &c., Broadcasting
(Offences) Act 1967

FOREWORD

There is a modern equivalent to the age old evocation *abracadabra*, and it is imbued with as much magical power. It is: *the sixties*.

In the sixties anything seemed possible and the period as a whole has been judged by the good fortune of a very small number of people. The explosion of activity related to the communications industry eclipsed most other events that could not be moulded into mass media hyperbole. The marriage of Princess Margaret to Armstrong-Jones became a real life Busby Berkeley film set. Whilst the emergent rock n' roll generation overpowered the loss of steam engines, birth of nuclear missile power, spy planes, earthquakes, the Wolfenden report on Homosexuality, African rebellions, a total eclipse of the sun, Russian dogs in space, volcanics on Tristan da Cunha, boy scouts wearing long trousers, Eichmann, Decimalisation, the end of trolley buses, Telstar, the Beeching Axe, the 'hot-line', the death of Harpo Marx, a whole host of independencies and international boundary changes.

There were a few events in the sixties that silenced the steady throb of rock n' roll, the deaths of Jack Kennedy and Martin Luther King, the enormity of Vietnam — itself made into a drug/rock opera — and a man on the moon. The music, the performers, recorders, presenters... all became part of an elite society that the rest of the world wanted to know.

That world was on the move, technology was keeping pace and in the midst of it all the good old 'wireless' became a tool for the new breed — a method of direct communication.

It is hard to imagine today just how accepted the Government control over radio broadcasting was. The very idea that ordinary people could produce a programme that would enter the privacy of an individual's home by means of a radio set was almost unthinkable. The pirate radio ships did it, they produced the programmes that people wanted to hear and they introduced a concept of radio broadcasting both new and vital. It swept Britain like a fever and the BBC would never recover that absolute authority again.

England's radio pirates were following a hallowed tradition. In 1925 Selfridges had sponsored an English language broadcast from the top of the Eiffel Tower on the subject of fashion, arranged by one Captain L.F. Plugge. It was this radio adventurer and his IBC (International Broadcasting Company), as *Radio Normandy*, that broadcast into the UK a whole variety of programmes featuring the leading stars of the day. It was a tremendous financial success.

The other substantial operation heard in the UK was *Radio Luxembourg* which began English language transmissions in June 1933. Despite endless bleating by the BBC, it was the war and Hitler that eventually closed down these popular 'foreign' stations. *Luxembourg* survived, as the home of 'Lord Haw Haw', and post-war, on into the present day; the IBC stations closed for good although the company survives and is still involved in the business of broadcasting.

Radio Luxembourg's domination of pop radio was only vanquished by the clear signals of the pirates with their non-stop selection of hit music, until then the crackling and fading from the Grand Duchy had been acceptable — better than nothing!

RONAN O'RAHILLY

Within the context of British Broadcasting, it was Ronan O'Rahilly, an Irishman, who led the way to free, independent, pop radio. It is easy to look back and think how obvious it was to put a transmitter ship outside the law, and promote the new craze dominating society — pop music. The mechanics of doing so were not so straight forward, yet no one at the time could have predicted the impact of *Radio Caroline* on the British public.

The station, it's personnel and it's owner became household names; it immediately spawned imitators around the coast of Britain, and they became important cogs in the ever greedy music machine. A hundred careers, forged aboard the pirate ships, continue today more successfully than ever, in other cases, the sudden exposure to fame resulted in a tragic aftermath.

Encouraged by the existance of *Radio Veronica*, O'Rahilly raised funds to secure the Fredericia and, in the Irish port of Greenore, owned by his grandfather, converted the former ferry to a radio ship. O'Rahilly, despite a wealthy background, had demonstrated commendable entrepreneurial skills in London with his record company, management operations and discotheque (the Scene Club). From the first test transmissions on Good Friday, 1964, *Radio Caroline* and it's survival became an integral part of O'Rahilly's life. Into the eighties, and with the 'Loving Awareness' message losing him listeners, Ronan O'Rahilly is as faithful to the 'Lady' (named after the daughter of President Kennedy) as ever. *Radio Caroline* and O'Rahilly, the softly spoken Irishman with a gentle nature and brilliant business acumen, will always hold a special place in the history of pop radio in the U.K.

SIMON DEE

The mercurial Simon Dee is also eternally branded as a pop pirate, although his stay at *Caroline* was relatively short. Erroneously described as the first voice on the pirate station (in fact, Chris Moore played the first music during tests) Dee actually introduced the first official programme with the words: 'Hello everybody. This is *Radio Caroline* broadcasting on 199, your all day music station'. Chris Moore then played the Beatles 'Can't Buy Me Love'.

After a year and a clash of personalities with Ronan O'Rahilly, Dee (Cyril Henty-Dodd) joined the BBC doing three different radio shows in addition to his twice weekly *Radio Luxembourg* spot. By 1966 Simon Dee seemed to be 'in'. Minor TV appearances like Juke Box Jury led on to his now infamous Dee Time, the result, so rumour has it, of Billy Cotton Jnr's faith in Dee. People watched, critics carped, and guests grinned. And ever so slowly the worm turned. Dee has an odd blend of aggression and charm in his manner, switching from one to the other quickly, and

LEFT: DEE WITH STUART HENRY
ABOVE: THE GOOD TIMES WITH DOGS

it's not one that endears people to him. Overnight he was 'out'.

Never has such a fall from media grace been so complete or so tragic. The newspapers were full for a time of Dee 'explaining' his problems until even these tabloid appearances dwindled to mere news items, tracking the self destruction of the man: Baliffs coming to take his furniture, speeding fines, fired from an Australian radio slot, jailed in Brixton Prison, left by his wife and children, assault; and losing two radio jobs before he even started them. The final ignominy for Dee was to be described as 'a vagrant' when he appeared in Court after an incident in Chelsea.

Today Simon Dee lives in SW London alone with his dreams, writings and fantasies and a reputation for being 'erratic'. At his worst he was no worse than many T.V. 'personalities' today. At best... he was a man of his time.

Pirate radio in Britain — twenty years old. For most people, including many of the DJ's involved, the time elapse seems hardly credible. It is ironic that on *Caroline's* 20th birthday the radio ship is once again an issue. In the North Sea, barely a spit of surf from *Caroline* is *Laser 558*, a station shrouded in mystery (sic). Rumours of the arrival of a third pirate ship to house *Wonderful Radio London*, are as yet just that, with the tantalizing hint that Mafia money could be involved. On land, radio pirates await the chance of legalisation via a licensing scheme.

And in the air... who knows?

**The Authors and Publishers
have agreed that royalties
from the sales of this
book are to be donated
to the Stuart Henry
Multiple Sclerosis Research
Appeal Fund.**

No book on the erratic radio pirate phenomena can be totally accurate or fully comprehensive. Two men on the same ship, at the same time remember the same incident in two different ways. A warm vote of thanks must go to the disc jockeys in this book who took the time and trouble to try and remember 20 years of radio life.

There have always been photographers and writers who had the intelligence and wit to record events long before 'the public' discover their importance. In the field of pirate radio we salute photographers: Martin Stephens and Dave Kindred. In the field of writing: Gerry Bishop (Offshore Radio); Paul Harris (When pirates ruled the Waves; Broadcasting From the High Seas); Mike Baron (Independent Radio); and a more recent study: Richard Nichols (Radio Luxembourg).

Special thanks to Mark Wesley and Pete Bowman for graphic material used in this book; Tony and Christine Prince for invaluable introductions; Gerry Merriman for original photographs of the leading D.J.'s; the artists represented by Popperfoto, Keystone and S & G whose work is used in this edition. To Anglia Television and BBC Radio 4 for access to their broadcast material.

Additional appreciation must go to Bill Harman, Dave Cowling and John Richardson for invaluable production work on Pirate Radio — Then & Now.

And finally: to all the warm hearted people who have offered facilities and support for this project, and to broadcasters, young and old, everywhere — thank you.

INTRODUCTION

There is no greater affront to the British Male than for an outsider to intrude and invade the privacy of his Club. It is immaterial whether it be *Whites* or the *Barnsley Working Men's Club:* the sense of outrage is a bond. Although superficially benign, at heart the BBC is just such a club, obdurate, ruthless, and at times petty. You may well imagine its reaction when, on March 24th 1964, it monitored some jumped-up radio station called *Radio Caroline* using 'its airwaves'. Pirate radio had struck and for the first time since Britain's leading dancebands had given live broadcasts from London's West End hotels three decades previously, the youth of the nation got what it wanted — continuous and almost unadulterated pop on records.

It was not entirely the fault of the BBC that this situation arose. Restricted by an anachronistic agreement with the record companies, it had limited airtime for records and had to fill in with too much dull and characterless music. In addition, the Light Programme had been trying to please most of the people most of the time and, as ever with compromises, it failed.

Radio Caroline South was followed swiftly by *Caroline North, London, Scotland, 390* and a number of 'one man bands', like *Radio Sutch.* They supplied an ever-increasing demand for over three years until the Marine Offences Act was passed on August 14th 1967. With typical British hypocrisy the Establishment had frowned but done nothing. Although illegal, the pirates were popular and it took time to organise something legal to replace them. Offices in London accepted advertising and the off-shore transmitters pumped out the message. The record companies which charged the BBC for using their product fell over each other to supply the pirates for free. Unofficially, record 'pluggers' took to the small boats and sailed to the off-shore ships to deliver their wares in person. The land was alive with the sound of popular and deliciously illicit music. Eventually it had to end, but not before it had created a 'new wave' of disc-jockeys modelled on the American style, friendly and informal who contrasted favourably with the actors, comedians and so-called musical pundits used largely by the BBC. *Radio London* introduced such names as Ed Stewart, Dave Cash, John Peel, Pete Brady and Duncan Johnson. *Caroline North* and *South* competed with Rosko, Simon Dee, Tony Blackburn and Kenny Everett. *Radio Scotland* came up with Stuart Henry.

It is ironic that these names formed the backbone of Radio 1 when, under irresistible pressure, the BBC brought Robin Scott over from their Paris office to head their own pop music channel in 1967. The battering they had taken had sharpened their wits, for it was a good choice. Now, most of these ex-pirates are respectable household names with TV series under their belts and are lucratively engaged in head-lining gigs, opening shops and appearing in commercials. In fact they are almost 'the old brigade', recognised and respected in the pop world for their contribution to British radio. I doubt whether they would have had the opportunity without pirate radio.

Today commercial radio is no longer a dirty word. But after just a few years it is in danger of becoming as stereotyped as the BBC was. Many of the stations are formalised and motivated by the demands of advertisers whose products are largely for the over-thirties. Once again the young are becoming restless and a new batch of pirates has emerged — *Laser,* emanating from New York, *Jackie* and, once again, *Caroline.* Now it is the turn of legitimate commercial radio to complain about their underground broadcasting. Nothing hurts so much as a hole in your pocket.

As the variety of communications media increases so the listeners become more voracious. The new pirates are here to assuage this thirst; to woo musical and ethnic minorities and supply their special needs. Are we perforce becoming the second greatest consumer nation in the world? Twenty million portable radios say we are.

Bunny Lewis 1984

1958

SUMMER A German fishing boat **Cheeta** is taken to a small port in Zeeland. Registered in Panama and owned by **Ib Fogh** (75%) and **Pete Jansen** (25%). Studios were built in Copenhagen to record programmes for the boat, Danish Law only forbidding the broadcast of material from land.

JULY 11 The Cheeta, 107

BRT, leaves port complete with transmitter and anchors SE of Copenhagen. Then moves to South of the island of Ven. Test transmissions start on 93.12mHz FM. using a directional antenna. The station call sign was **RADIO MERCUR**, broadcasting between 6 am and midnight to Denmark.

JULY 17/18 Cheeta loses

her anchor and drifts towards the Swedish coast, running aground outside Malmo. Damage is caused to the aerial mast and transmitter and, after the salvage vessel **Karl** tows the radio ship into Limhamm, divers inspect the faults.

AUG 2 Repairs complete, **Cheeta** returns to position and recommences broadcasting.

AUG 5 The Danish government asks Panama to withdraw **Cheeta's** registration.

AUG 14 Panama threatens **Cheeta** with a loss of registration if broadcasts do not cease.

AUG 29 Panama disclaims the **Cheeta**.

The Danish Government, confident on the failure of **RADIO MERCUR** sits back to await it's demise.
Banker **Alex Thomsen** joins the company and advertisers look on the project more sympathetically.
The frequency is changed to 89.55 mHz to avoid interfering with a Swedish station.

AUG 31 Power is increased and an experiment in Swedish is broadcast (noon-2pm) as **SKANES RADIO MERCUR.**

Complicated plans are put into operation to obtain a second ship. It is hired from Baltic Panama Shipping Co. (London) by Internationale Radio Mercur Anstalt (Switzerland). The latter fits the radio equipment and then hires the completed ship to **RADIO MERCUR.** The new 450 BRT vessel is renamed **Cheeta II.**

THE CHEETA (THE FIRST *RADIO MERCUR* SHIP) AND (INSET) ANNOUNCER GITTE MÜLLER

1959

OCT 15 Radio dealers in Amsterdam meet at the Krasnapolsky Hotel. **RADIO MERCUR** is discussed and it is decided to launch a similar project for the Netherlands. Vrije Radio Omroep Nederland (VRON) is formed by Messrs. **Oswald, Lewin** and **Slootman** and registered in Lichtenstein.

NOVEMBER Swede **Jack**

Kotschack and Americans **Gordon McLendon** and **Bob Thompson** devise a plan to bring commercial radio to Sweden. The search for a vessel is on and they look at a tug **Herakles**, but decide it is too small. In Kiel, West Germany, they locate the **Olga**, a cargo boat built in 1921 as a three masted schooner. In 1927 her length had been increased from 98

to 134 feet and engines installed. Her previous name, the **Margarethe**, had simultaneously been dropped in favour of **Olga**. The first steps in launching **RADIO NORD** are thus taken.

DECEMBER 16 Test transmissions are heard in Amsterdam from **RADIO VERONICA**. Actually the transmitter is in the Office of

TOP: THE CHEETA II HOME OF *RADIO SYD*. BELOW: THE CHEETA II SAILING TO ENGLAND TO AID RONAN O'RAHILLY 1966

one of the directors but this secret is not revealed. The effect of the test is to generate a lot of local interest.

1960

The ex-German lightship **Borkum Riff** is bought for conversion by the **RADIO VERONICA** team. Parts being shipped across the Dutch German borders are stopped by the Dutch. Meanwhile a second fake broadcast is issued from an island on Lake Loosdrecht.

EASTER Borkum Riff leaves Emden, towed by the **Guardsman**, an English tug. She anchors off Katwijk ann Zee, Holland. **RADIO VERONICA** begins test transmissions on 1620 kHz (185 meters) and reception is noted over sixty miles away.

MAY 6 **RADIO VERONICA** begins serious regular transmissions and the Dutch Government use their installation at Nordeich to jam the pirate. **VERONICA** moves to 182 meters — out of the range of most radio sets. The station is receiving massive press coverage of its activities.

MAY 13 **RADIO VERONICA** ceases transmissions.

MAY 15 **RADIO VERONICA** appears on 192 meters with better reception.

MAY 31 The Olga enters Hamburg to become a radio ship. Chief engineer of the conversion is 73 year old **Dr Pepke,** Capt. **Kaj Hallonsten** acts as consultant. The original plan is to have two masts of 125 feet with a looped antenna but this is rejected in favour of a single stem. Work progresses slowly and then a hitch occurs.

JUNE Panama withdraws its protection from **RADIO VERONICA** which is re-registered in an undisclosed country.

AUG 10 A Hitler-ite law prohibiting the installation, repair or operation of a radio station without government permission is evoked by the authorities to frustrate the proceedings. The Olga, now renamed the **Bon Jour** leaves for the free port of

Copenhagen. Nordhava-Vaerftet erect the ariel and two 10KW Continental Electronics 316B crystal controlled transmitters are flown from the USA in 6,000 loose parts for re-assembly.

NOV A survey shows RADIO VERONICA has an audience of 5,000,000. Advertisers refuse to be impressed and the original shareholders bail out leaving three of the remaining directors (**Dirk, Jaap** and **Bull Verweij**) to run the station. The plan is to improve the service and cut down on overheads. Recording is done on a kitchen table and the records are the announcers own.

DEC 20 6pm: The Bon Jour leaves Copenhagen bound for anchorage near Stockholm. Supplies were to come from Nynashamm where the nearest Customs post was situated although it is inconveniently distanced down the coast.

Two and a half hours after sailing the Captain drops anchor because of fog. The boat is half way to its destination in the freshening wind when it is noticed that the stays of the mast are working loose. **Bon Jour** anchors off the island of Gotska Sandon to carry out repairs.

DEC 23 11am: The ship gets under way again and eventually anchors in what the Captain thinks is the correct position. The transmitter is turned on and a blue flash comes from the ariel — all goes dead.

DEC 24 The fishing boat Danette, with the special Christmas tapes on board finally locates the **Bon Jour**, who is not anchored at her correct position, after a two day search.

CHRISTMAS DAY The crew abandon ship in fear of the mast collapsing due to a heavy sea, a pilot boat takes them to Sandhamn.

DEC 26 The salvage tug **Neptun** picks up the crew and returns them to the ship which is still in one piece.

DEC 27 The Bon Jour is towed into Sandhamn. The Captain suggests that they go to Lidingo for repairs but on arrival find that the ship had closed down six months previously. The **Bon Jour** sails for Stockholm and a new, better qualified Captain: **John Johansson**. To avoid any legal difficulties she sails onto the Crichton Fulcan yard in Finland, whereupon the Finnish Government pressure the yard to refuse the work. With the **Bon Jour** anchored out in Chalk Harbour the shipyard send a team out to repair the ship afloat.

BELOW LEFT: THE BORKUM RIFF. BELOW: *RADIO NORD'S* SHIP THE BON JOUR. (INSET) *RADIO VERONICA* ON BOARD THE BORKUM RIFF

TONY BLACKBURN

RADIO CAROLINE
RADIO LONDON

LUXEMBOURG
RADIO ONE
RADIO LONDON (IBA)

Tony Blackburn is one of the most experienced presenters on the airwaves. His technique of broadcasting has covered many styles, some of which have earned him eternal opprobrium from some sections of listeners. Blackburn, however, operates on a far different level personally than might be indicated by his various radio 'acts'. Recently leaving *Radio 1* after 20 years, some reports say fired from *Radio 1*, Blackburn has made his IBA *Radio London* soul and funk show a cult leader. If you transpose 'innovative radio' for 'pirate radio' then the illegal broadcasters have no greater supporter than Blackburn. It all seems a natural progression for the man who started out as a musician and singer . . .

"I went to a Public School called Millfield, then to college, Bournemouth College of Technical Education, got a Higher National Diploma in Business studies. At the same time I was playing with a dance band as a professional guitarist.

I read an advertisment in the New Musical Express wanting disc jockeys for *Radio Caroline*, I applied and got the job, simple as that.

It was already on air, I joined round about a month and a half after it started. I was on *Caroline South* and stayed out for two years.

I started off doing a programme called The Big Line Up at 4 o'clock in the afternoon, then started doing the breakfast show on *Radio Caroline*. Then I joined the pirate ship *Radio London*.

I thought it was a superior operation, it was a better signal, and had proper American made jingles, I preferred *Radio London* very much."

The transition from a live performer to the anonymity of the microphone booth suited Blackburn, and still does, although not everyone likes his brand of freeform chat. Perhaps more than any other DJ, with the exception of Tony Prince, Blackburn is hip to contemporary pirate stations and their aims, many of which he supports in a real way.

"I find radio very natural actually, I prefer it. I prefer talking to a microphone more than an actual person, I still do, it is more interesting.

I saw a documentary on *Radio Caroline* on ITV, but I hadn't heard it very well, because I was living in Poole in Dorset and it didn't really get in there. I wanted to get onto *Radio Caroline* so that I could get closer to the record business and make records — that was the idea of it, but it turned out I did better as DJ.

I am very proud to have been a part of that era because we really did revolutionise the whole of the broadcasting system. It was much more interesting to be a part of it then than probably now, because it has all been done and I think when the *Marine Offences Bill* went through pirate radio, certainly *Caroline,* lost its direction a little bit and has never quite regained that magical quality because there are more radio stations around now.

The reason why it did so well then is that everybody was starved of entertainment because there was only the BBC; there was no commercial radio and a terrific lack of radio, whereas there is now more radio around, not enough, but more and a single station doesn't have the same impact.

If it hadn't been for them (the original pirates) we wouldn't have radio as we know it in this country still, because the BBC would have held onto their monopoly. The pirate radio stations that we have now, the landbased ones like *Horizon* and *JFM* particularly, are very important because they eventually... in five or six years time they will influence the way radio goes. I am convinced *Horizon* and *JFM* won't go away, legislation won't get rid of the idea and eventually we will have 24 hour soul radio stations and not just the pop ones."

Tony Blackburn became part of the personality DJ cult that projected pirate presenters into well known celebrities virtually overnight; a state of affairs his own career has sustained, so much so that his marriage break-up became front page news. Blackburn reflects that the station itself is more imporant than the presenters, although the two would seem inseparable...

"Once again that side of it was important as well, but the main thing was that the stations themselves *Radio Caroline* and *Radio London,* they were the main thing. But through those stations you did get big personalities like **Kenny Everett** and various other people, and the interesting thing now 20 years on you are getting personalities coming from them again. Certainly pirates have altered and they are going for more music because the legal radio stations talk so much. The legal radio stations are waffling on so much, the IBA and BBC for that matter, they are losing their audience by loads of talk.

Laser is an interesting one, *Laser 558,* they are getting a very big audience, they are worrying *Radio 1* and *Capital,* they are worrying everybody.

Luckily though they don't worry me so much because I am doing a different type of music, but certainly if I was on a commercial radio station I would be very worried. But I don't think we have got proper commercial radio over here yet."

While the youth of Britain was dreaming of becoming a *Caroline* DJ, Tony Blackburn actually left to join the ship next door, the Galaxy and it's Americanised programming:

"I listened to *Radio London* on test, when they came on I immediately wanted to go, they had a better format, better Top 40 radio format, which I have always used and still do to this day.

Tony Windsor approached me as we were going off *Radio Caroline,* the tender used to go from *Caroline* to *Radio London* and eventually took in *Radio England* as well, then go off to Harwich. We were parked alongside *Radio London* and **Tony Windsor** said 'if you want to make a move and come to us, we'd like to have you'. He said 'if you are interested' which I was, he said 'go to Curzon Street', which I did.

They wanted me to change my name to **Mark Roman** and become a part of the Roman Empire as they put it, I didn't like that idea very much, so I said 'no' and they said 'in that case we are not interested'. Later they said 'o.k. come under your own name'.

We weren't doing all this loving and awareness business, that was later on, personally I don't see the point of that. It doesn't really come across very well. When I listen to it I think some of the DJs are a bit baffled by it all. They don't quite understand what it is."

Despite a sympathy for his old employer and a certain loyalty to the station ID, Blackburn confesses to seeing the eclipse of *Caroline* by the more progressive stations on the pirate airwaves.

"I think the thing is it has become established a little bit and *Lazer 558* has a better name to it, it is more up to date now. I must admit I have listened to *Radio Caroline* lately and it has certainly improved a lot..."

By the time the Marine Offences Bill became law Blackburn was already marked down as BBC potential and he left *Radio London* for a job with the official broadcasting company, his being the very

ANOTHER 'FUN' DAY IN THE LIFE OF A RADIO DISC JOCKEY

first voice to be heard on the virgin *Radio 1*:
"I thought it was tragic to leave, but by that time I had been offered work on the BBC and I thought having been out there three years I didn't want to spend the rest of my life on the North Sea, so I took the job with the BBC.

I think to be fair with **Johnnie Walker**, one of the reasons why he stayed out there was he hadn't been offered a job on BBC. I do think those who were offered jobs would have gone for it like a light because they, like myself, saw the fact that the game was coming to an end."

Actually, the job was on the Light Programme with a view to going on *Radio 1* eventually. It was an obvious move to make, apart from anything else, you can't spend your whole life at sea, unless you want to be a merchant seaman.

Johnnie might have had the principle, when I opened up *Radio 1* there was a certain feeling of excitment about it but at the same time a certain feeling of resentment. I thought the BBC had benefitted rather strongly from pirate radio, I always looked on *Radio 1* as a bit of a compromise anyway.

It wasn't as exciting and it didn't have the family feel of *Radio Caroline* or *Radio London*, particularly with *Radio London*, that to me was the best station on the air and it's namesake still is."

Blackburn had been selected for the new BBC operation and so it is not surprising that his face fitted pretty well into the scheme of things. He found no difficulties with the methods ashore or the hierarchy system inherent at the BBC, with only minor exceptions:
"Yes, the transition was very good. The people at the BBC I liked very much indeed in the early days, they were very helpful and it was a trial period for all of us and they very sensibly said 'we'd like you to help us out, because we don't know as much about it as you guys'.

I found it difficult to come to terms with the producer, I could never quite understand, in fact to this day I don't understand why it is a pirate radio station that is broadcasting music the same as *Radio 1* does it without producers and *Radio 1* needs a whole host of producers, I've never understood what they do.

I think it is an old fashioned system. I can understand having producers for programmes like I am doing now at *Radio London* when there is more speech involved. *Radio 1* is a juke box like the pirate ships, in fact there is not so much involved in running *Radio 1* as a pirate ship, because they don't have to have logging systems for commercials, but you can easily run radio without producers. You need a programme director and an assistant and that is it."

Like so many others *Radio Luxembourg* became a part of Blackburn's career, albeit a small part, although it was primarily from Hertford Street, London . . .

"I was doing shows for EMI and a little bit for Decca in the days when it was recorded. I had been out to *Radio Luxembourg* but I never broadcast from there, except I am one of the very few people to broadcast from the *Radio Luxemborg* studios for *Radio 1*. Because we did some programmes for *Radio 1* when the EEC thing came about and we did a programme from *Luxembourg* and I used the *Radio Luxembourg* studios and I used the bell they have as well a few times."

Blackburn is reported frequently now stating his interest in actually running a radio station in a management capacity. One thing he has learned from the BBC experience is to steer clear of the overburdening officialdom that infests large corporate structures:

"When I say officialdom, it wasn't bad, it was good fun, the people there were nice. I just felt the way it was operated could have been updated a little, I felt it was a little bit BBC I suppose. I think the problem is they have a staff system and nobody can lose their job unless they bring the BBC into disrepute, so they have to use people somewhere. I think sometimes they use people in jobs that have got a bit outdated now.

If I was starting up a pop radio station now I would not employ producers, I certainly wouldn't employ the mass they do, you need producers for news programmes, but when you have programmes just playing records, I don't think you need those people anymore.

I have a sympathy for the pirates, I would like to see the American broadcasting system in this country. In London I don't see any reason why we shouldn't have 50 or 60 radio stations if they are run commercially and if they are not under IBA authority. I wouldn't see them under the IBA or the BBC, they would have an overall authority that would dish out frequencies and the power that you broadcast on and any complaints that come in they would deal with, but they wouldn't tell anybody what to broadcast, as the IBA do now.

I would do away with all the red tape because I think the system we have at the moment is ruining radio. In other words the reason why *Capital Radio* and IBA stations have become so dreadfully boring, leaving out local BBC radio for the moment, is because they have the monopoly and it is not good to hold a monopoly. Also some of those stations, particularly *Capital Radio* which has the monopoly of London, which is ludicrous, it is trying to be all things to all people and in this day and age you cannot do that, you have to specialise a little bit more.

Laser 558 is very good and there is no reason why it shouldn't be there, if it makes money why let it not go ahead, but legalise it and bring it to land. The trouble is when you bring these things to land and make them legal

IT'S THE WINNING SMILE THAT DOES IT

there are so many restrictions like needle time. I would do away with all those ridiculous restrictions, come to a different agreement, try and do away with needle time restrictions, which don't apply in America. I would suggest to the record companies, the publishing people and broadcasters that we all charter a few planes go over to America, listen to it, learn from it and bring the whole system over here. That is the way it should progress, and if two people want to put on a radio station and they have the money to do it and the wavelength to do it then go ahead. Doing away with all these monopolies, particularly the IBA . . .

I am very much in favour of local broadcasting, not national so much, because local broadcasting can do much more and be more interesting and if it is done properly as has been proved by *JFM*.

With my programme on *London* where I specialise in jazz funk and soul music, that is the way to go about it, by all means have your Top 40 radio stations as well, but you also have a Country and Western station, an all day religious station if you want to and if you can make money out of it. People don't have to listen, but it has been proved if you give people choice, in America, the more you have the bigger the cake becomes, because people actually tune in and do away with their tapes.

If for instance *Horizon* or *JFM* went off the air I wouldn't bother tuning into radio, because there is nothing there for me, I would just go to tapes.

TONY BLACKBURN AT *RADIO LONDON (IBA)*

But it will happen, it is just that we are very slow in this country, but we do need the pressure of pirate radio stations in my opinion. This is something totally abhorrent to the authorities I know, but they are my views and I don't go along with the authority view at all."

Blackburn still sticks with his micrphone although there are occasional forays into television, the obvious music shows and so on. He has an interest in a cable franchise and is still looking into the management concept . . .

"It is not a question of resisting TV, but not being asked to do it much.

I am doing *Sky Television*, which is a cable thing, which goes to the continent and I do an hours pop, jazz funk, actually it is a soul and dance music programme, using videos. I do things like Punchlines and these sort of things. I did 10 years with Top of the Pops, I've done a lot of television actually.

Essentially I prefer radio, because it interests me more and I know more about it. What I would really like to do is to run a radio station now, that is what I am aiming for, although I love broadcasting and the reason why I haven't tried to go into that side of it seriously is I still enjoy talking nonsense, but I would like to run one and also broadcast a little on it."

Some people might be surprised to find that Blackburn is well aware of the restrictions some of the his radio gambits impose and he feels that his readiness to progress proves that no trend is irreversible, no image immutable:

"That is why I have resigned from it, I felt that *Radio 1* for me had lost it. I felt the programmes I was doing on *Radio London* were far superior than *Radio 1* and I didn't want to be heard nationally.

The reaction I was getting in the country... when I appear in London and the South East the reaction I get is that people come along for a good laugh and I feel quite good, I think *Radio London* is the best broadcasting I have ever done. Whereas I did a couple of discos outside the London area and you get people coming up and saying 'woof, woof, where's Arnold?' and I thought 'this isn't me anymore'.

I asked *Radio 1* when **David Jensen** left if they would like me to do a soul programme for them and I asked for a soul programme but there wasn't the time slot

TONY BLACKBURN ON *PIRATE RADIO LONDON*

available. I tend to think they concentrate too much on rock, but I felt this was the time to jack it in. I also wanted time at the weekends to be able to travel abroad for Sky Television, so I needed the time and I had done four years of seven days a week, and I am a bit tired and you need to refresh your brain a little.

So I thought I would go back to what I enjoy doing and that is soul music and local radio; but I would like to have the national exposure again doing a soul programme because I think it is sadly lacking.

Quite honestly, if I lost the job here I wouldn't rule out the idea of going back to the pirate ships.

If it got to a stage where radio over here was so terribly boring I would certainly open up a pirate radio station tomorrow, but I hope that is not necessary because I don't think that is the way we should go. The way we should go is to legalise; instead of trying to ban the whole time the authorities should look at it and say 'why is it doing so well', look at it and try and bring it into a system. But I am also very much in favour of young people coming into it and unfortunately whenever you read 'getting rid of the old guard', I am afraid it is the old guard that are controlling the stations. This is why it doesn't move forward because the people who are controlling needle time, wavelengths etc., are all old men now and it is time we got younger people with new modern ideas."

Tony Blackburn is, however, grateful and mindful of his own introduction to broadcasting via the illegal pirate stations and still believes that those with the spunk to broadcast this way have a very real contribution to make. He at least is still prepared to tune in to that...

"Yes, I am very proud to have been a part of that type of broadcasting, because funnily enough I think the bigger personalities were bigger then than they are now, one of the reasons I think being that we had the gumption to get up off our arses and go into the North Sea.

Current broadcasters haven't had that experience, I think some of them are very good, but we do have one or two people broadcasting on *Radio 1* at the moment certainly wouldn't survive, because they haven't got big enough personalities.

So I am proud to have been a part of that era, the early and late 60s era, at the same time, unlike some of the guys who I still meet at reunions, they seem to have lost the fight, I am more rebellious now than I was in those days, I am glad to be a part of the cable era.

I'd love to be a part of bringing about the advent of the specialist stations in this country, not community radio stations so much, I have a dreadful idea of stations that do nothing else but talk about brownie packs and I hope they don't because nobody would listen. But I would love to be asked to be on some Committee looking into broadcasting because it is terribly simple to modernise it, a part of the people that kick the system up the arse, because that is what it really needs at the moment."

1961

19 year old Ronan O'Rahilly arrives in London from Ireland: 'I looked on my move as a challenge'. He founds an Actors Studio based on the very popular 'method' acting of **Lee Strasberg**. Soon after **O'Rahilly** founds the Scene Club in Great Windmill Street, Soho; which later promotes embryo R'nB bands like the Rolling Stones.

JAN 31 The **Cheeta II** starts broadcasting on 88mHz. The equipment from **Cheeta I** is installed and airs Swedish language programmes on 89.55 mHz.

FEB 4 The **Bon Jour** sets out for a new attempt to set up station.

FEB 6 The **Bon Jour** anchors off Orno whilst a gale lets engineers go through

ABOVE: RONAN O'RAHILLY FOREVER *THE* RADIO PIRATE. LEFT: THE *RADIO NORD* SHIP AND JACK S. KOTSCHACK, OWNER, IN THE FOREGROUND

final safety checks and then she goes in search of a more equable location. A loud crack from the mast announces that the insulators have broken.

FEB 7 **Bon Jour** limps into the Finnboda shipyard at Stockholm, new insulators are fitted and complete checks carried out. The transmitters are turned on for seconds at a time and at night a three hour test is made with the boat right in the middle of Stockholm harbour. The

authorities' seals on the equipment, put on when the boat entered Swedish facilities, are cleverly by-passed.

Dual channel stereo using both transmitters is given out from **RADIO MERCUR**. **Bon Jour** experiences interference at night caused by **RADIO LYON** operating on 498 meters and so changes its broadcast frequency to a more satisfactory 602 kHz. Listeners, however, having being bombarded with publicity telling them **RADIO NORD** was on 606 kHk (495 meters), are left in the dark about these finer tuning ideals. Supply is brought down to a fine art with a tender, the **Listerlind**, being purchased, and even an aircraft to drop cannisters into a clever system of ropes and hooks astern.

FEB 16 The first ever pirate broadcast for English audiences emanates on 192 meters from the CNBC (Commercial Neutral Broadcasting Co.), based aboard the **RADIO VERONICA**. It can be heard from Hull to Margate between 5am to 7pm daily, latterly 8am to 1pm. The DJ's are **Bob Fletcher, Doug Stanley** and **Paul Hollingdale**.

FEB 21 **Bon Jour** anchors and begins tests on 495 meters (606 hKz). Within a few days trouble with condensers forces a return to Finnboda.

MARCH 1 **Bon Jour** is back at sea and testing.

MARCH 2 The Swedish Government announces that any radio ship in Swedish waters will have its equipment confiscated.

MAR 8 Now re-registered in Panama and with a ship re-named (yet again!) the **Magda Maria**, official programming of **RADIO NORD** begins at 10am and finishes at 6pm

MAR 9 **RADIO NORD** opens for business at 6am

JUNE The **Nijmah Al Hazz**, a Lebanese freighter, is fitted out in Belgium with an American antenna and German transmitter.

JULY **Cheeta I** goes to Norway for repair work.

SEPT 15 The 240 ton **Nijmah Al Hazz**, is renamed **Lucky Star** and transmits as **DCR** (Danmarks Commercielle Radio) to Denmark on 93.97 mHz FM between 3pm and 11pm. Anchored in the sand off Copenhagen it is run by disgruntled senior staff of **RADIO MERCUR** who have disagreed with the **RM** desire for profit at the expense of programme quality. Programmes are pre-recorded in Copenhagen and feature a mixture of light music and serious stuff like opera and plays. It does not prove to be a popular balance.

SEPT 29 The Danish Post Office orders that coastal stations can only handle distress calls from radio

ships, all other traffic is to be blacked. **RADIO MERCUR** has used **LYNGBY RADIO** to transmit talks for **Cheeta II** to rebroadcast.

Danish Prime Minister, **Viggo Kampmann** is interviewed for an appeal on behalf of handicapped people, broadcast by **RADIO MERCUR**

Advertising revenues and popularity increase for **RADIO VERONICA**. Staff salaries are paid promptly and English language broadcasts are tried out using an English team, and known as CNBC. This project soon dies out due to the increasing dominance of **VERONICA**.

NOV 25 **Cheeta 1** anchors in a new position (between Fyns Hoved, Furnen and Reerso, Zeeland) and recommences output on 89.58 mHz. Shortly after the aeriel collapses. The two ships change places and **Cheeta 1** anchors off Copenhagen.

DEC 2 A storm from the S.W. attacks **RADIO NORD**.

DEC 6 **RADIO NORD'S** storm is now a 70mph gale and the **Magda Maria's** anchor drags. By 11 am the ship is adrift but broadcasts continue until 5pm when everyone on board has to man the ship to keep it afloat. The engines are restarted in the nick of time. At midnight broadcasting ceases and the **Magda Maria** staggers into Sandhamn.

DEC 8 Repairs are complete and the authorities waive confiscation on the basis the vessel would have been lost if she had not come in. **Magda Maria** leaves in dense fog to take up position and the team leave the Government seals on the equipment as a joke, having by-passed them with ease.

1962

O'Rahilly representing **Georgie Fame**, tries to get air time for the artist. Major labels of the day (EMI, Decca, Pye & Phillips) will not help and **RADIO LUXEMBOURG** is committed to 'booked' time by the same 'big four'

RADIO MERCUR begins regular news bulletins (7am and 7pm lasting around 5 mins each).

JAN 29 **RADIO MERCUR** and **DCR** (Danmarks Commercielle Radio) merge. **Ib Fogh** resigns and his share split: 60% **MERCUR** and 40% **DCR**. It is announced that in 1961 **MERCUR** had a turnover of 6,000,000 Kroner.

FEB 12 **Cheeta 1** puts out a distress call during a gale and is towed into the Langelinie Quay, Copenhagen. Police detain her and the ship is declared stateless. She is sold to **Mrs Britt Wadner** who is responsible for the Swedish programming on **MERCUR**. The **DCR's** ship **Lucky Star** takes over **RADIO MERCUR** broadcasts on 88mHz

Mrs Wadner puts the newly acquired **Cheeta 1** to sea, anchors off Malmo and starts up on 89.62 mHz FM as **RADIO SYD**.The Government decide to alter their Halsingborg FM station in order to overpower the weaker signal but hours

before the move **Mrs Wadner** alters **RADIO SYD** to 88.3 mHz FM

MAR A mystery jammer blacks out **RADIO NORD** each evening. The station complains to the Swedish Telegraph board. It mysteriously stops.

MAR 29 The Swedish Parliament introduce measures to outlaw offshore radio.

MAY Swedish anti-pirate measures are passed to become law on August 1 along with other Scandinavian action against off-shore radio.

JUNE 14 Third reading of anti-pirate bill in the Danish parliament. Result 83 for, 38 against and 23 abstain.

JUNE 30 **RADIO NORD** closes down despite plans for a light music service on FM and a Top 40 format. After lying at anchor **Magda Maria** sets sail for the North Sea.

JULY 3 A ministerial meeting is held with Denmark, Norway, Sweden and Finland

agreeing to unite on enforcing the new laws.

JULY 10 **RADIO MERCUR** aboard the **Cheeta II** is shut down and the ship sails to Elensburge in W. Germany to be sold to **Britt Wadner**.

JULY 31 Scandinavian anti-pirate measures become law at midnight. **Lucky Star's** transmitter shuts down at 11.55pm.

AUG 1 Swedish law aimed particularly at **RADIO NORD** comes into force.

AUG 2 The **Magda Maria** arrives at El Ferrol in Spain from the Baltic.

AUG 13 5.00 pm: Transmission from **Lucky Star** appears using the old **RADIO MERCUR** tapes. The old manager of **RM** announces that his company only hired the boat and denies responsibility for the new output. The owner of **Lucky Star** is said to be a Guatamalan **Senor Louis Arturo Delboso**.

1963

AUG 16 Armed Danish police board the **RADIO MERCUR** ship and discover it is un-registered. Customs escort the radio ship into port and it is impounded pending the appearance of the owners. There are no arrests. This seizure results, elsewhere, with the withdrawal of backing from **Alan Crawford** and his Project Atlanta.

AUG 27 **THE VOICE OF SLOUGH** 65 foot former fishing vessel, The Ellen, expects to leave Scotland for its permanent station in the Thames Estuary off the Nore. It has three one-kilowatt transmitters, capable of a coverage of at least 80 miles.

SEPT 14 The Magda Maria sails from Spain giving a destination of Dover, England. Magda Maria now becomes re-named the **Mi Amigo**, to be one of the most famous names in the pirate ship story. business.

Alan Crawford, with associates ex-Major **Oliver Smedley** and **Kitty Black**, starts planning Project Atlanta. **Smedley** sets up a host of interlinking companies in Lichtenstein and Britain. Property developer **John Delaney** has promised £70,000 but declines after hearing news of the arrest of **Lucky Star** by the Danes.

OCTOBER **Britt Wadner** is fined for breaking the new laws regarding off shore radio broadcasts. **RADIO SYD** has been using the better equipment from **Cheeta II** including a 7KW Siemans transmitter. **RADIO SYD'S** popularity is illustrated by the 10,000 members of its listeners club.

JAN 11 The Mi Amigo (previously called the **Magda Maria**; previously called **Bon Jour**; previously called **Olga**; previously called **Margarethe** — in that order) enters Flushing and gives the owners name as: Messrs **Amatra**, Vaduz, Lichtenstein.

JAN 15 Mi Amigo leaves Flushing but puts into Brest on January 19th with damage to the steering gear.

JAN 26 Mi Amigo sets sail to Galveston, Texas, via Las Palmas.

MAR 9 The Mi Amigo is in Galveston being prepared for a refit as a luxury yacht.

MAY Eleven sponsors are fined for taking time to advertise on **RADIO SYD**.

DEC 18 **Allan Crawford's** Project Atlanta secures funds to purchase (at last) the **Mi Amigo** and she leaves Galveston for El Ferrol, Spain, via Las Palmas.

THE LUCKY STAR, HOME OF *RADIO MERCUR*

EMPEROR ROSKO

CAROLINE SOUTH
RADIO ONE

LUXEMBOURG
VARIOUS (USA)

Twenty years after *Radio Caroline,* **Emperor Rosko remains the ebullient rapid fire character that made him a household name. Rosko, real name Mike Pasternak and son of Hollywood director Joe Pasternak, works mainly in the USA now and it is not easy to remember just how his American presentation took the virgin English radio waves by storm.** *Caroline's* **own Wolfman Jack still prefers to zap his listeners:**

"**Stuart Henry** was the only one to get sea sick and ended up faking his show, and pretending he was out on the boat... and on coming out of the Navy and four years at sea already, I was the one that was least affected by the movement of the waves. I went to *Caroline* in the South, I was on there about a year, and then I went to *Radio Luxembourg,*

they wanted to adopt what I was doing, so it worked out rather well."

As a French speaker Rosko worked with *French Radio Luxembourg,* **a move that didn't worry him too much as 'the wages went up 600%' and although hard headed about the broadcasting business, he does admit to a slight feeling of being part of that exclusive club...**

"A bit, I mean it was that way but not above all other things, you would still be competing with jocks on the station, everybody trying to outdo each other, but if it was a matter of us against everybody else, you play your poker game and you go out to win. For example when *Radio England* started we stole their jingles and in order to do that we had to monitor their test signals, so of course it meant everybody had to put extra hours in, but it was sheer pleasure.

The minute they started testing, their DJs were so wanky, they'd play a record then there would be three seconds of silence then a perfect jingle through. The night before they were going on the air we had all the jingles nicked and it was a collective effort, we edited their name out and put our name into a very expensive jingle package and nobody knew but the guys on the ship that we had done this. So as they went on the air the next day, we went on the air using their jingles with our name in them and I understand they just about died in London.

On the other hand, if you went into town to work say the *Caroline Night Out* you would do your best to be better than anybody else on the ship."

The Rosko view of life doesn't include nostalgia for the past, due to the fact that his involvement with the pirate ships happend well into a career that included Europe and Australian radio. He wasn't asked to join the relaunch of *Caroline* in the early Seventies with the advent of the new wave:
"No, they knew better, nobody in their right mind would go out there because there is basically nothing going on. I don't hold much hope for them, they might stay on the air but they won't make any money. They are staying on the air because of some radiotronic philanthropist who is supporting it. I started in the Navy and in the early days I had radio experience of the type they were trying to do. They had their experience coming from European and Australian Radio.

Caroline never shut down, *Caroline* has been on the air even since the boat sank four years ago, it has just been broadcasting over on the Dutch side but you can hear it. When *Caroline* started there was only BBC and maybe *Luxembourg* that was any kind of competition and it was them versus the pirates. Now you've got 40 stations plus *Radio 1* going 18 hours a day, they will not have a chance.

Simply because it was new, that was the special ingredient and also it was a little bit illegal, it wasn't real broadcasting, if anything it was quite the opposite, it was really Mickey Mouse. Real broadcasting is doing it with proper equipment and taking incoming calls etc.

It was difficult sometimes playing records when the boat was at 60° angle but I don't think that affects what you could call real broadcasting. Certainly it was easier in a way because you had so much more to talk about, what went wrong, what went right and the daytrippers were coming out, it was just novel, and because it was novel it was exciting, and because you had a bigger audience.

They were a training ground for *Radio 1* DJs, who have now became *Radio 2* DJs."

The Emperor spent his time at sea with complete confidence that he was aboard the style leader and he only begrudgingly acknowledges that nearby *Radio London* came up to scratch. Other pirate ships around the coast get short shrift . . .
"I would only be aware of those on station whose signal was respectable and *Radio Scotland* was this poor little tiny signal by our standards. People would write to me from Liverpool saying 'we heard the show for a little bit', I know they couldn't hear us regularly, but our signal basically went right up to Ireland, but not on a regular basis. I have never heard of anybody that heard *Radio Scotland* except the people who lived next door to where the thing was transmitted, but I couldn't have cared less, you could hardly hear those little tiny transmitters they had on the forts. All together the pirates were in one respect if you are analysing it, it was only *London* and *Caroline* and all the rest . . .'"

Rosko was cautious when the Marine Offences Bill became law, minding his position as an American citizen, but a new direction to his career wasn't something to be worried about. Rosko doesn't share some of his ex-colleagues nostalgia for the close-down . . .
"Some of us need those kind of memories to get us into our twilight years. There was **Dave Lee Travis, Tony Blackburn, Tommy Vance, Norman St. John.** I don't remember **Simon Dee** being on there. Two guys who went to Australia, they were really good but I don't remember their names.

I met **Stuart** *at Radio 1. Radio 1* was coming on to play pop music and the *Radio 2* DJs at the time, with the exception of one or two, weren't really suited to *Radio 1*. The strip shows were mainly done by producers and the weekend boys did their own subject, to some mild form of abuse if we took advantage of it.

It was a whole new ball game, with that came the first mobile discotheques and roadshows and things which I pioneered, I think I was probably the first roadshow in the world in the strict sense of what it finally evolved to as todays gargantuam system."

The flexibility the radio pirates had enjoyed at sea didn't exist in the BBC, however, and there was certainly supposed to be no dabbling in politics as *Caroline* had done in an effort deflect the Marine Offences Bill:
"The BBC, we can make fun of them in the pop department, but they are still probably the biggest and best radio station in the world. It is a little known fact and I am sure it is true, that the **Ted Heath** Government would never have come to power if it hadn't been for *Radio Caroline* who devoted a certain period for three months prior to the election to 'Vote in the Conservatives', because they were going to legalise pirate radio. He started gaining from the day that started being broadcast.

I liked *O'Rahilly*, a good chap actually. I don't see him anymore but I used to be fired regularly by his partner for not playing his payola records and Ronan would hire me back every time. I would say my integrity comes before your profits and he'd say your fired, then two days before I was due to go back I would go and see Ronan to say goodbye, and he'd say hired, your hired, and this would go on all the time.

Then they started getting this other system together, with a guy called **Robby Dale**, he was out on the boats and has gone on to Holland, they made him chief DJ and responsible for playing payola records and it got a bit more difficult.

In the beginning I would just wait for them to come aboard and as soon as I saw the package of records I'd throw them in the ocean before anybody saw them. Even though no one else did it I'm sure everyone sympathised because nobody really wanted to play some of the stuff that was sent out, although sometime there were some good ones in there and you would have to be fair. But that they could make more records than I could throw away there is no doubt about it.

If someone had sat down and said this is the only way the station can stay on the air maybe I would have seen it differently, but the way I saw it, it was just someone profiting off my integrity."

As an ex-Navy man Rosko had no problems with the shipboard systems whereby the Captain is in absolute charge of the vessel. Although some DJs found it hard to relate the two seemingly alien factions jammed so closely together for weeks on end, the Emperor was more involved with the never ending ratings war . . .
"We ate together, but the day to day running of the ship was left to them. In our thing we were always trying to figure out how to deal a severe blow to *Radio London*, the only other station that mattered in terms of UK competition, and that took a lot of our time.

We once came together and had a thing when **Henry Cooper** fought **Ali**, I think it was the first time, and that was being broadcast exclusively on BBC Radio, that is what they kept saying; we told our listeners not to worry because the BBC was lying, and they didn't realise *Radio Caroline* also had the rights to the Cooper/Ali fight. A total lie and I guess in London (they could reach us occasionally by relaying a message via someone on the coast who had a ham radio) there was a frantic series of messages. I had a scheme up my shirt which was this: we taped each round from the BBC, edited out any mention of BBC and about 3 minutes after they had broadcast, inserted our parts. The illusion was complete and we broadcast the whole fight then afterwards gave an after fight commentary.

A boat would be very carefully scrutinised before coming alongside, as a collective we thought about it (security) a little bit, but it is like: do you think the invasion of Poland will reach England?

The good times were all the bird dogging around, that was a great period for pop music and girls and the economy of the country was still in a fit of socialism gone mad, there was money everywhere, the pound was worth $3, it was a great period."

Like many of his ex-shipmates Rosko has broadend his base to encompass more than radio presentation. Passing fashions of the seventies left him feeling flat and he reacted by taking a sabbatical in his native California:
"The only thing you get trapped by is perhaps your style, but I do lots of jobs, I'm a record producer, I manage a group in California. I have done all kinds of things, almost a music publisher and hope to be again soon.

I faded a little bit in '76, there were too many other pressures and it got monotonous, when punk music was coming in real strong and I wasn't relating to it at all. I needed a break, I didn't take holidays. In those days the Rosko Roadshow was doing five or six shows a week, cranking up 2000-3000 miles a week, that went on for five, six, seven years, all high speed aggravating work. Between that and *Radio 1* I just thought: off to California for a bit."

Rosko arrived on the scene as a radio man and continued to be one, although there was a high fail rate on presenters who were forced ashore . . .
"I don't think they disappeared by choice, because they came in and they didn't sustain for whatever purpose, some weren't good enough, some fell ill, maybe nobody would hire them so what else do you do, you go back to doing what you were doing before.

Radio 1 started with 28 disc jockeys from which at least 22 came from assorted different ships, **Keith Skues** I vaguely remember had something to do with the forts, like I said he is not on *Radio 1* any more, last I heard he was running some commercial station somewhere. **Johnnie Walker** is at *Radio Wiltshire*. **DLT** was a good mate, **Tony Prince**; **Michael Ahern**, that is one gone to Australia, I rated him as probably the best breakfast disc jockey in Europe at the time, he didn't get what he wanted at *Radio 1* and Australia was a viable option and was home. Canada and Australia were the only two other possibilities of getting any idea of what was going on in rock and roll radio after America."

Some of the young radio men who launched offshore broadcasting on the unsuspecting public in that halcyon summer regarded themselves as part of a select club, not so the irrepressible Emperor. His relations were purely businesslike:
"If someone had said to me villains had raided *Radio Scotland* and shot three disc jockeys I would have felt very badly about it and I would then be keeping a much sharper eye out, but that never arose. The only way you would look at another DJ is if you were going to go do another gig somewhere and they said they had already booked so and so.

Caroline started off as what was known as the *Caroline Night Out*. The *Caroline Night Out* was a mobile discotheque setup, speakers had been put up on tables and twin decks and we played records, we had one or two groups but mainly the DJs spent a half hour each playing records with the kids, we got paid I think £80 which was damned good money in those days and from that came the idea of: take a rig and put it in a van and do it ourselves, who needs *Radio Caroline* and hence was born the roadshow, which now exists everywhere."

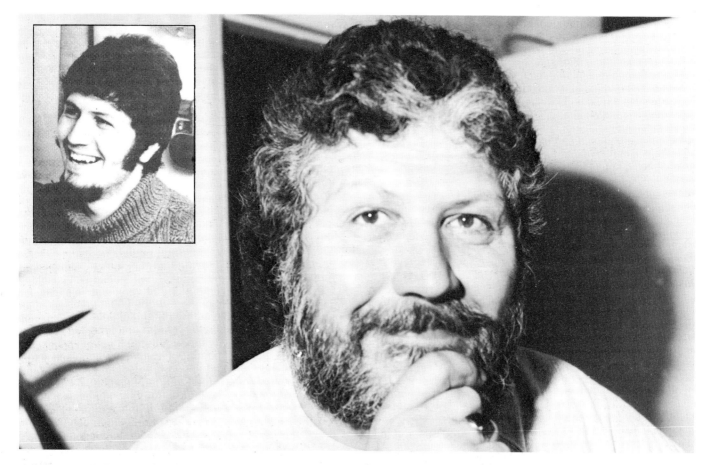

DAVE LEE TRAVIS

**CAROLINE SOUTH
RADIO ONE**

Dave Lee Travis has come a long way since he toured with his homemade music console, generally remembered as 'the monster', around the Northern clubs. Dave's warm and sympathetic radio personality made his transition to television a natural career progression; and his lifelong love of photography resulted in a highly successful series on the subject. One of the most liked of presenters, DLT's popularity has sustained since his launch into broadcasting on *Caroline South***. The pioneering trail from Manchester to the** *Mi Amigo***, however, has a familiar ring to it . . .**

"I was born in Buxton and the only reason I was born there was because my father didn't have enough bus fare to carry on to Manchester and had to stop over night, that is the only link I have got with Buxton really. I moved almost immediately after I was born. I was dragged screaming on the roof rack of an Austin Seven at a very early age to Manchester, which is really my childhood home. In Manchester — I realised that disc jockeying was what I wanted to do. I had always been a bit mad and I worked as a designer when I left school, designing for some of the stores there and in my lunch hours I was going round to a club called *The Oasis* which was in Lloyd Street, Manchester. It was really one of the great small clubs of the 60s and they had a Dansette record player. Eight records on and one would clank down, this was what DJs were in those days.

I went there selecting records, then eventually

started talking to the punters in the afternoon; then I got a job one night a week then two nights a week — at £1 a night incidentally. I think that fired my enthusiasm and eventually I made the break away and went professional as a DJ and the first place I went professional was a *Mecca Ballroom* in Burnley, Lancashire, where I was working six nights a week and getting £13."

DLT's touring show, with equipment, became a hit on his circuit in the Manchester area, and the huge system was a constant source of interest...
"It was actually one of the first DJ consoles of its type because there wasn't any about. People had never heard of two record decks, they'd say 'what the hell do you need two for, why not one' and that was the attitude because nobody knew of twin decks. I actually built this myself literally from the ground, not that I was the greatest as far as electronics was concerned, but then there wasn't much to think about in those days. The thing was driven by a 30 watt amplifier — for Christ's sake, you wouldn't use that on a single stage speaker now. It is crazy, but in its day people used to think it was great. I used to pack it in the back of a mini van and away it went.

The Oasis was the first club I worked at. I had the pleasure of introducing The Beatles for the first time in Manchester at the club and always remember being quite taken aback when I arrived for the evening to find, a couple of hours before the place opened, queues four deep out of Lloyd Street into the main centre of Manchester right to the Town Hall and all the way round the edge of the square. I thought 'no way are all these people going to get in the club'. That is when I became aware of The Beatles popularity.

From there on it varied I went on to *Mecca* again, *The Plaza* in Manchester, and then pirate radios.

The interesting thing there was that I decided that pirate radio was a good idea for me, the way I went about it was quite fun because I found the address at 6 Chesterfield Gardens for *Caroline* and the Canadian guy **Bill Hearn** was the man in charge at the time. I always remember: I have a saying that I tell other people 'it's all right sticking your foot in the door, anybody can stop people and impress them for a moment but you have to have the clout to follow it through'.

I thought I had what it took to be a DJ on *Caroline* and went into the office at Chesterfield Gardens and I remember being fascinated by the fact that it was one of these very old buildings with a ceiling twenty odd foot high and the guy's desk was sitting there, behind his desk there was a wall twenty feet long loaded with shelves of 5" spools of tape. When I walked in I knew that they were all would-be disc jockeys, so I thought 'no way am I getting on the end of that queue'. I did the interview bit and chatted with him he said 'fine Dave, we'll get in touch'; and that was the moment in my career that I turned it all round. I said 'you'll have to forgive me but I want to do

you a sample show downstairs'; they had this little studio in the building. I really pushed and did them an on the spot demo. Within days I was on the ship."

There had been an interlude in DLT's career that was the result of his friendship with Peter Noone, known at the time as Herman of the Hermits. This comprised of a trip to the USA and a chance to become an ersatz James Bond...
"The thing that was interesting in the States was that I hadn't done any radio work at that point, but I had done quite a lot of club work and it became known that I was a DJ. At the time it was 'anything from England was great' and a guy called **Gordon McLendan**, who I believe is still going in the States, got in touch with me in Texas and wanted to offer me a job. You can imagine I had not been on radio at all so it was very tempting and he was offering me a job in the States on his station. He wanted me to take the name James Bond.

He actually said to me 'I'll supply you with an Aston Martin and a bunch of girls to follow you around in public' just for the James Bond image. This sounds ludicrous now, but at the time the Americans were in love with that and I think it was a fairly important decision in my career to say 'no'.

So I knocked that on the head thinking how nice it might have been to be running around the States in an Aston Martin and came back home. That is when I got the job at *Caroline* and then of course I spent two years on the South ship; I left and was asked back to go on the North ship which I did for six months, then it became illegal and I quietly disappeared back off to Manchester."

As befits DLT's exuberant personality, he found life aboard ship exciting and stimulating and was the butt of much good humoured leg-pulling for his habit of wearing a red rose buttonhole. For Dave at least, it was a magic time:
"It was under way yes, but not *well* under way, there were lots of people applying for jobs. The reality of life on the boats was exciting, exhilarating — because it was something totally new. All we had been used to was the Light Programme and very little pop music and suddenly there was somebody walking along saying: 'hello fellows here's a bit of adventure for you, we'll put you out on a ship in the North Sea, you can eat Dutch food, you can be sick over the side and you can play the sort of music all the kids want to hear'.

Of course it was all very vague in those days, the bosses didn't know what they were doing, all they knew was they wanted something other than the Light Programme. It was a training ground, very much so, for all of us, but the actual life on the ships. After the initial few months of euphoria you settled down to it like you would in any job, familiarity breeds contempt; we all loved our jobs, but the actual life on board the ship could be a bit trying.

The funniest thing of all when you think about the

ship first of all it has a 200 foot mast, secondly it's anchored at one end and there is this most amazing pendulum effect. If it was a normal ship floating in the water and it rode the waves, that is one thing; but when it is tied down at one end with a bloody great mast swinging to and fro, in a force 7 or 8 gale, you really knew you were moving. Everything went, the food off the tables, and you had to do everything like that. You had to watch the television like it, if you were into television and could get a decent picture, you tried to read, you tried to eat, sleep, play records and try and sound enthusiastic... and all the time you are swaying back and forth. It wasn't always like that but the times when it was, it was horrendous. And then of course the great summer months, it was like a mill pond.

For the first six months I thought it was an exciting project, certainly something different; after the first six month period I personally started to think 'this is going to be history without a doubt'. Then I suddenly felt pleased that I was part of it because it is of great historical value to the music scene in Britain.''

The developing business interest in pirate broadcasting as a means to make money was introducing an undesireable element into the picture, on board Caroline **these events were viewed very much at a distance and the jocks, as with all jocks at sea around the coast of England, did not involve themselves with the management of the station.**
"I don't think anybody on the ship ever thought there was any real danger of being attacked. There was always the knowledge that the coastguard were spying on us — but I don't think anybody every really felt threatened.

There are certain things in your life that have a long standing effect on you and that is one of them. I can't remember what magazines I was reading in my bunk at any given time, I can remember odd things about it, probably the things I want to remember. I can remember everybody on a Sunday charging round a radio set to listen to Round the Horn, which was one of our favourite programmes and little things like that. I can remember having a news flash handed to me by one of the newsreaders at the time through a porthole inbetween his toes. He was on top deck sunning himself and he decided to drop a news flash and this foot appeared while I was broadcasting. We called him the Big Toe after that. I think his name was **Mark Hammerton**, he just had this piece of paper between his big toe and second toe and stuck his foot through and I took it off him. The most stupid things happened on the ship really.

Caroline was the first, the original, and I think probably if everybody admitted it, thought 'we're Caroline to hell with the rest of them'. Not that we weren't interested, because suddenly along comes a more Americanised station. At the time it was crazy, nobody could handle it at all, we couldn't work out what they were trying to do on Radio London but it had its success there is no question about it.
Then the original is usually the best.''

With the Marine Offences Bill to cut short DLT's pirate career, he took the unusual step of returning home to the North, despite a radio following that would have stood him in good stead at the BBC...
"**Johnnie Walker** and **Robby Dale,** they both stayed on. I thought 'to hell with it, we've done our bit now, we've got to go peaceably'

I actually just came off with the rest of them and the one thing I always remember was that when we left the ship, within a week of that, most of the guys had gone to the BBC to try and get jobs. I knew that was going to be the case and, being a lone ranger type that I am, I thought 'I'm not getting on the end of that queue'. I disappeared quietly back off to Manchester not thinking about London.

After I had been home for about three weeks and trying to work out what the hell I was going to do next; very low key and quietly I put my head round the door of a fellow, who shall always be dear to me called **John Wilkes,** a producer in Manchester, and introduced myself. I said 'I've been on the ships for 2½ years and thought I'd let you know I'm around should anything come up' and left it at that. Within a couple of weeks he had come back to me to say that **Ray Moore** who had been doing this programme Pop North was going down to London to join the staff down there, would I like to try it, and I said something to the effect of 'is the Pope religious'.

I started on Pop North which was a great programme, a live lunch time show and I sang with the band and John let me have my head which was great. From that developed all the other programmes through to Radio 1 stuff.''

Although the early days on the ship had been free and easy, DLT had come ashore with a real working knowledge of professional programming:
"There were free hands at first and then suddenly somebody in the background got tied up... **Phil Soloman** who had Major Minor Records, he certainly had an adverse affect on the ship, apart from anything else we were playing The Batchelors once an hour because they happened to be on his record label, that was plugging to the wrong degree. So I mean I never liked him.

Probably, nowadays, we would be a little more selective in programming material, first of all you have to think about not clashing with the guys either side of you, secondly you think more in terms of a good balanced programme for your listeners. At the time I think we all went for the music we particularly liked, we just pulled them out of the library and threw them in. There is a lot of argument to say that maybe that is the way all programmes should be put together.

I fitted in very well because like everybody else you imagine the BBC to be... as a kid you get this image of broadcasters wearing bow ties on radio. Obviously you start forming opinions — suddenly you get there and there is a guy your age who is producing. Although it wasn't

A pirate station aiming nationally, or even at a portion of the nation I don't see a reason for. A community station which will maybe cover the area of Tottenham or some other area a small area, maybe that is valid. Maybe we are getting into cable vision, almost the same way as cable is trying to aim for a set audience maybe there is room for radio doing that thing. But then we are talking about another thing entirely because cable television and localised radio to a degree have the same sort of problem and that is the more there are, the more watered down it is going to be. Personally I think at this moment in time with four channels and the fifth channel being the video machine, I think we have a good selection of television. I think when cable starts to operate properly there has to be a drop in standards.''

always that way, but *Radio 1* realised very quickly that they had to get young guys in and not the old staff; but basically they had the right sort of people at *Radio 1* producing and they got on very well with the jocks.''

DLT balances his affection for the old days with a professional assessment of the value of illegal broadcasting today. He still rates the influence of the pirate boats highly but considers it, essentially, a job well done . . .
"I think it *was* extremely important, I think without it *Radio 1* would have come about but it would have been at least five years later, at the earliest, before anything else seeped through. At some point somebody would have realised there was an American way of radio, which is not quite the British scene even now, but it would have got kids bubbling and thinking about it. But I think in essence *Radio Caroline* was a kick up the arse for the broadcasting system in Britain.

In my honest opinion, at this time there is no point whatsoever to pirate radio. The only point there would be is if its trying to be *more* creative. If we all fell into the category that the Light Programme did in its very early days and got very stifled and certain types of music didn't get enough airing, maybe then pirate radio would need to kick us up the backside. But I don't think that is the case.

If you listen to *Radio 1* now the freedom in terms of music on *Radio 1* is incredible and local stations and commercial stations all know what they are doing now. Therefore what is the logic of a pirate station sitting out there saying 'the BBC is all rotten and commercial stations are rotten and we are great'.

I think there is no place today for *Radio Caroline*. He had an idea once and I would think that it would have been more logical to carry on with than this. He was going to have a pirate TV station in an aeroplane flying round, that would have been great.

I have heard 20 minutes of *Laser* in total so I can't form an opinion, but I have had people phone me and say 'have you listened to this, it's good', but I haven't really had time to form an opinion.''

DLT is a big man, this presence matched to his undeniable charm and humour make him a natural for television and he is one of the minority of presenters who can come from behind a studio microphone to stand before a camera — more difficult than might be imagined:
"I love TV, I have always been an avid photographer and it has only recently come out that I am doing it seriously, in terms of a book, at the moment.

If somebody asked me which do I like more — radio or television, I couldn't answer, because they are totally different parts of the media. I do like radio because you are using your brain all the time and conjuring up pictures with your voice and you have that warm repartee with the audience. Television is a totally different thing in that you might be saying something that could be taken the wrong way on radio but there is no question when they *see* the smirk on your face that they know what you are talking about. I've done all sorts of things on television now apart from the photographic thing, which was one of the best shows for me personally. I enjoyed it thoroughly because it was something that I really love, photography, and to get a programme is just an added bonus to me. I am doing it again next year incidentally, so that was a great thrill, but yes, television I love.

I keep doing appearances on like *Punchlines* and I go loopy on there and do strange things. I like it, it's good fun, but I love radio as well. At the moment I am doing a Saturday programme 10am 'till 1pm which was a positive move on my part, a year last April, to allow me to do more television. I had been on a daily programme for 11 years.

I thought the time had come because I had to refuse so many TV shows because, invariably a TV company wants you for a couple of days somewhere and I couldn't do it because I had to keep being back for the radio programme. So it is not at the cost of my radio programme, it is just the way my work life has developed that I feel more comfortable now doing one show a week on *Radio 1* and having the time to move about, produce ideas for TV, do my photography and it is just a comfortable way of working for me now.''

1964

The Dutch government actively look for a way to silence RADIO VERONICA after being impressed by Scandinavian action.

JAN 30 The Mi Amigo arrives in Las Palmas after nearly sinking en route from Texas.

FEB 5 The Mi Amigo docks at El Ferrol in Spain for strengthening and repairs.

FEB 6 Postmaster-General, **Ernest Bevins**, is questioned in the House of Commons regarding the rumours about RADIO CAROLINE. He replies with hints that legislation would be introduced to deal with such an eventuality.

FEB 13 The ex Danish passenger ferry **Fredericia** leaves Rotterdam for Greenmore. 702 tons, she has a hull specially strengthened to resist ice. Planet Productions has rented the vessel from the Swiss firm of **Alranne** to be converted to a radio ship — RADIO CAROLINE.

FEB 15 The Mi Amigo sails for Greenore, Eire (calling en route at Corunna), to have a new radio mast fitted.

Ronan O'Rahilly and **Allan Crawford** run neck and neck in an effort to be first on air. **Crawford** has been planning longer, but **O'Rahilly's** father, a wealthy industrialist also owns his own port in Eire—

Greenore. Both parties' vessels use the facilities there to equip although bad feeling is caused when **Crawford's** Mi Amigo is forced out to anchor in the harbour mouth to make way for **O'Rahilly** senior's freighters. Rough seas almost scupper the Mi Amigo, saved only by prompt action by her skipper.

MAR Britt Wadner of RADIO SYD is fined in Sweden for illegal broadcasting.

MAR 26 CAROLINE sets sail from Greenore to anchor the next day off Felixstowe. Test transmissions take place on 201 meters (1495 kHz).

MAR 28 Noon: RADIO CAROLINE starts regular transmission on 197 meters (1520 kHz) with The Beatles 'Can't Buy Me Love'.

MAR 29 Easter Sunday: The official launch of RADIO CAROLINE with **Simon Dee** announcing 'Hello Everybody. This is RADIO CAROLINE broadcasting on 199, your all day music station'.

APRIL 3 The Mi Amigo, planned to be the home of RADIO ATLANTA is still in

Greenore port in the Irish Republic for fitting a radio mast. She has been competing with **Ronan O'Rahilly's** boat for services.

APRIL 7 Panama withdraws recognition from CAROLINE.

APRIL 21 12.30am: RADIO ATLANTA is off Lands End sailing for her anchorage when a loud crack denotes a broken radio mast. The 141 foot swaying aerial affects the steering and the Mi Amigo has to enter Falmouth for repairs, she arrives at 3pm.

APRIL 27 RADIO ATLANTA anchors off Frinton-on-Sea, Essex, in rough weather. This prevents technicians getting aboard to begin transmissions.

APRIL 30 The Peterna puts broadcast staff aboard Mi Amigo.

MAY An ambitious project gets underway launched by Reklame Exploitatie Maatschoppij (REM), led by ship builder **Cornelius Verolme**. Their plan is to build an artificial island at Verolme's dockyard in Cork and set it up off Noordvijk, in

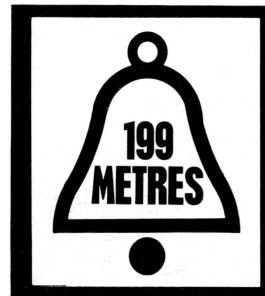

I LOVE CAROLINE ON ONE-NINE-NINE
CAROLINE CLUB
RADIO CAROLINE
LONDON, W.1

Holland. From here a radio and TV station are to broadcast, **RADIO & TV NOORDZEE**.
The island, to become known as REM island, is to be sunk onto the sea-bed like an oil rig, with its legs in concrete.

MAY 9 **RADIO ATLANTA** begins tests on 197 meters after **RADIO CAROLINE** has shut down for the evening. This is an attempt to cash in on **O'Rahilly's** ready made audience and therefore publicise the new station. DJ **Bob Scott** emphasises to the audience 'This is a test transmission only'.

MAY 11 The Postmaster-General claims he has received complaints from the Belgian Government about interference from **RADIO CAROLINE** with the official Brussels station, on 198½ meters.

MAY 12 6pm: **RADIO ATLANTA** begins regular programming on 201 meters (1493 kHz). Broadcasting is to run from 6am to 6pm, extended to 8pm within a short time.

MAY 26 **ATLANTA** announces she will pay royalites for music played on the station to the Performing Rights Society.

MAY 27 **RADIO SUTCH** goes on air from **Shivering Sands Tower** transmitting on 1542 kHz (194 meters), it is owned by pop singer **Screaming Lord Sutch**. The first record played is 'Jack the Ripper', by the stations owner.

MAY 28 Officials from the Ministry of Defence, along with members of Kent Police start out for **Shivering Sands**, but are recalled en route.

THE M1 AMIGO (*CAROLINE SOUTH*) AT GREENORE AND, BELOW, THE FREDERICIA AT ANCHOR (*CAROLINE NORTH*)

JUNE 3 Test broadcasts start from **RADIO INVICTA** — based on **Red Sands Fort** in Thames Estuary. The station is owned by **Tom** and **Frances Pepper**, and is managed by a Canadian, **John Thompson** —formerly associated with **THE VOICE OF SLOUGH**.
INVICTA tests on different wavelengths, from a 750 watt transmitter.

JUNE 21 As part of Leeds University rag week students attempt to launch a pirate station from the yacht **Carmen**, off the coast from Harwich.

JUNE 24 Mr Jeremy Thorpe is given leave to introduce a Bill, under the "10 minute rule", to regulate the placing of advertising on television and radio. He complains that **CAROLINE** just 'sings like an off-shore siren'. A radio station he says 'could just as easily be inflammatory, seditious, obscene or undesirable, with no protection to the public'.

JULY 2 RADIO ATLANTA (Project Atlanta) and **RADIO CAROLINE** (Planet Productions Ltd) announce the merger of the two stations. **O'Rahilly** and **Crawford** will be joint managing directors. Of the two ships — **CAROLINE** will re-anchor five miles off the Isle of Man and broadcast **RADIO CAROLINE NORTH** on 199 meters. The **Mi Amigo** will stay where she is broadcasting to London and the South East from Frinton-on-Sea and become **RADIO CAROLINE SOUTH**, also on 199 meters. The various departments of the two organisations will merge into one and the **CAROLINE CLUB** will extend into the new areas reached by the stations.

8pm: **RADIO ATLANTA** ceases to exist.

JULY 5 A station calling itself **RADIO FREE YORKSHIRE** broadcasts in the Bridlington area. It is operated by prospective local councillors, who are doing it so they claim, 'to demonstrate the damages of pirate radio'.

JULY 12 RADIO RED ROSE plays from aboard the steamship **Red Rose** about 20 miles from Liverpool. At present the broadcasts last only a couple of hours, but it is hoped to get the station going 24 hours a day.

JULY 13 CAROLINE, under the command of Captain **Hangerfelt**, anchors off the Isle of Man. **RADIO CAROLINE NORTH** continues broadcasting on 197 meters from 6am to 9pm. **MANX RADIO** complains to the Post Office

BEFORE AND AFTER: THE GALAXY AS *RADIO LONDON* LEFT: SCREAMING LORD SUTCH AT HOME

about their 50 watt FM signal being affected.

JULY 17 Regular transmissions begin from **RADIO INVICTA** on 985 kHz, centred on the London area.

JULY 19 First tests begin from **RADIO NOORDZEE** on 1071 kHz (280 meters). This is to change to 1400 kHz (214 meters), where it stays.

JULY 29 First programmes in Dutch begin from **RADIO NOORDZEE**. They last from 9.00 am to 6.15pm

AUGUST **RADIO SYD'S Britt Wadner** is sentenced to one month in jail for repeatedly breaking the off-shore broadcast laws. A big support demonstration follows. As prisoners are allowed to carry on their profession in custody,

Britt records programmes in her cell at Hinseberg Prison (!)

AUG 15 First test transmissions begin for **TV NOORDZEE**. They continue through the next week, and attract a massive audience in Holland.

SEPT 1 Regular transmissions begin from **TV NOORDZEE**. It proves extremely popular with the Dutch public, and advertisers flock to it.

SEPT 16 The Dutch Government, considerably less enchanted with **TV**

NOORDZEE, begin a debate in Parliament on the issue.

SEPT 17 Cheeta I runs aground near Malmo, this results in a hole below the waterline.

SEPT 19 Midday: Cheeta I is towed into Malmo for repairs to be decided upon.

SEPT 30 **RADIO CITY** begins transmissions from **Shivering Sands Fort** on 1261kHz (238 meters). It was formerly **RADIO SUTCH**, and is now owned by the pop star's manager **Reg Calvert**. Lack of funding from advertising forces **Calvert** to

take on a number of religious broadcasts.

AUTUMN **RADIO VERONICA** introduces their Top 40 and in addition live broadcasts begin for the first time from the ship.

OCT 7 Evening: Cheeta I sinks at Quay 11, Malmo, Sweden.

OCT 22 The Galaxy, the former minesweeper **Manoula** sets out from Miami. She is 185 feet and 780 tons.

NOV 19 The Galaxy, now renamed **RADIO LONDON** arrives in the Thames Estuary, and begins broadcasting test signals, on various frequencies, (412 meters and 324 meters). It is warned by **CAROLINE** boss **Ronan O'Rahilly** that it is

inside territorial waters, so it moves position.

RADIO LONDON is owned by Marine Investments Inc., with offices in Freeport, Grand Bahama. It is managed in London by Radlon (Sales) Ltd, headed by **Phillip Birch**. He is ex-army (attaining the rank of Lieutenant in the Royal West Kents) and spent some 15 years with **J. Walter Thompson**, working on the Ford and Kodak accounts. Its own press release sums its aims:

"The Station format: The responsibility for programming and presenting 'Big L' lies with the programme director. He works on the principle that people like packaging, and uses the system of 'Formula Radio' and Top 40 format. Formula broadcasting has been tried and proven all over the world, in fact wherever there is commercial radio. The programme controllers job is to present to the average British listener, and to adapt it to the public's taste. The conclusion so far has been that people want — and are getting — the top forty records in Britain. This, however, does not mean that **RADIO LONDON** churns out from 1 to 40 in the **RADIO LONDON** 'FAB 40' throughout the day. The system works like this: Selected records from the hit parade are played together with revived records, a new release and an overseas hit or track from an L.P. On the half hour there is a newscast and weather forecast with time checks at various intervals. This method ensures that no record is played more than once in the three hour programme presented by each disc jockey, and the Top 40 are only heard five times in any one day, and the 30 American or L.P. tracks are not repeated that day. There are six minutes of advertising each hour, and each three hour programme takes its name from the disc jockey."

DEC 5 Further test transmissions are heard from **RADIO LONDON** on 265, 266 and 277 meters medium wave, with a power of 17Kw.

DEC 12 The Dutch Parliament passes a law outlawing broadcasts from structures on the sea-bed.

DEC 14 **TV NOORDZEE** closes down, and ownership of the station goes to a British company, while the island itself now belongs to Explitacion De Construciones Maritima Excomarsa based in Panama.

DEC 16 **Tom Pepper** (real name: Harry Featherbee), co-owner of **RADIO INVICTA**, along with DJ **Simon Ashley** (real name: Barry Hay) and engineer **Martin Shaw** drown when Pepper's 36 foot launch capsizes after bringing supplies to **Red Sands Fort** from Faversham.

DEC 17 REM island is boarded by the Dutch police, and **RADIO NOORDZEE** is closed, and its equipment is confiscated. The Public Presecutor of Amsterdam, Dr. Hartsuijker, explains that this action was a result of the stations refusal to comply with the new law.

DEC 23 **RADIO LONDON** begin regular transmissions.

RED SANDS FORT (*RADIO 390*) AND, INSET, SHIVERING SANDS FORT (*RADIO CITY*)

PAUL BURNETT

RADIO 270
LUXEMBOURG
RADIO LONDON (IBA)

Paul Burnett has lost none of the sparkle and charm that showed in the publicity blurb for the launch of *Radio 270*. **Almost typically, Paul got a berth with the pirates by one of those lucky breaks that seemed to be so common in the early days. His background, however, was conducive to entertaining and he took the usual path of disc jockey-ing outside his normal working day:**

"I was born in Manchester, parents variety artists, so consequently I went to about 12 different schools, summer seaside resorts, winter with a pantomime or circus; great childhood but disastrous academically. But as it turned out great grounding for the kind of job that I ended up doing.

My parents separated when I was about 10 so I didn't have anything to do with the business at all until I left school at 15 and went into a big department store in Darlington, then I joined the Air Force in 1961.

Five years in the RAF and two years in Aden and it was then I started radio. 20 years ago this month I just did it as a hobby in the evening, like guys doing hospital radio, so when I came back to this country in 1965 the pirates were in full swing. I sent an audition tape down to *Caroline*, was asked to go down and see them, and it is funny how things happen I didn't get the usual photostat, I got a letter from **Ken Evans** who was looking after auditions then and he virtually promised me the next vacancy that came up I'd get a job.

I promptly showed that to the Manager. I was in the RAF at the time being DJ at the *Top Rank* in the evening and I showed it to the Manager, he showed it to the local press who did a thing on 'local man joins *Caroline*', really a bit premature, because I hadn't got the job, from that somebody saw it and told me about this new ship that was starting and one thing led to another, I went up to Newcastle for audition.

A funny thing is I got so used to doing the DJing in the evening and the RAF during the day I began to feel the RAF was the hobby and the DJ was the main part and I accepted the job and said I would be ready to start in January 1966, forgetting I had another six months to do in the RAF. It hit me as I was walking to the railway station. Bless my mother, she cashed her premium bonds in to buy me out and I started work on pirate *Radio 270.*"

Despite the fact of being in the right place at the right time, the spirit of the age very much contributed to Burnett's break into commercial radio. Getting on air today is a very different story as Paul is quite ready to admit:
"I started doing it in the RAF as a hobby and found it was just terrific, I love sitting by a microphone with a stack of records and going through. I feel a bit sorry for lads because it has become a 'respectable' job now; they want 'O' levels and 'A' levels and all the things, it is regarded as a form of journalism. So guys going into local radio, which seems to be the route now, I think it is a shame because the extroverts... you can't define personality, you can't teach anybody that you either have it or you don't."

Radio *270* at Scarborough was a very popular local station, run by local business interests who enjoyed a certain popularity too. Although not an early arrival on the pirate scene it did operate with some sort of professional standards...
"I was with it from the beginning, which had its moments, because what happened was we were supposed to go on the air on 1st April 1966 but on that morning of the most almighty storm blew up. One of the worst in living memory off that coast. The consequence of that was it wrecked the boat, we had 150' mast 100' of it came down and was dragging down to the bottom of the sea and it had to be cut away. At 1966 prices £10,000 of aluminium mast went down to the bottom of the ocean and is there to this day as far as I know. That put us back a little, three months later we went on the air and I was with them until six months before the end.

I hold the not very admirable distinction of being one of the few broadcasters to actually throw up reading a commercial out, it was for the boss' Supermarkets, he had a special offer on Danish bacon and I had the breakfast show and was supposed to be describing 'mmm can't you just smell it frying in the pan', and the ship was rolling around so much I couldn't reach the button to turn the microphone off and I just vomitted all over, which was not very conducive to buying bacon.

I was a terrible sailor and I got used to working with a bucket between my knees. You do learn to live with it, Nelson was a terrible sailor, you learn to work your way around it, you know you are going to be sick so you go to the toilet. I did four hours in the morning and four hours in the

afternoon because the rest of the time we were just swanning around on the boat bored stiff.

Looking back it had its romance, it was sordid, you lived in dreadful conditions and all the problems that arise with any bunch of blokes cramped together under those circumstances, friction and whatever. But terrific cameraderie and the moment we stepped ashore suddenly all the hideous part of it became a memory. I would feel so ill, because the boat taking you from ship to shore was even worse, but as soon as one got on shore from feeling like death, five minutes and you felt on top of the world. I thoroughly enjoyed it, initially it was two weeks on and one week off, which was dire — we are talking about a really small boat . . .''

Local success didn't do anything to dispel the sheer impact the two style leaders in the South, *London* and *Caroline*, had on the regional jocks:
"We felt envy, that is all we felt, you knew **Kenny Everett** and **Cash** and **Blackburn** and on the other ship of course **DLT** and **Prince.** You knew they were on a big ship with their own cabins and you felt nothing but envy and you hoped you would end up on them. But it was so short lived it never happened. I got an offer of a job on *Manx Radio* which was much less money and much harder work but I took it because I figured that come August when the Bill went through there would be hundreds of jocks looking for jobs.

Funnily enough on the day I got that I also got the offer of a 13 week contract with the new *Radio 1* but the other one was a six month contract. I often wonder what would have happened if I had taken that job, like a lot of them were with *Radio 1* for the first six months and then they were filtered out. I'm glad I did it the way I did because I would have missed out on some great years with *Radio Luxembourg.*"

Manx Radio had a very good pedigree, its operators often at odds with the mainland Government and this independent spirit had a lot in common with pirate broadcasters...:
"When I joined it, it had just moved from a caravan on the sea front and it was run by a guy from a South African station, a very go-ahead guy, he thought come the pirates closing down he wanted them to go for a National commercial radio station. I think they should have done that because the island survives on tourism and what *Caroline North* did was to tell everybody about the Isle of Man. They had great years when that ship was going apart from the income from commercials and so on. But they didn't because they are subsidised heavily by the British Government and were frightened of losing that. It would have taken courage but I think it would have been a good move, that is my opinion.''

Paul Burnett didn't sit it out for the Marine Offences Act to sink the Scarborough radio ship but it remains an important part of his career:
"I left in March '67 and I have a grudging admiration for **Proudfoot**, he is a very hard man to work for, he demands total loyalty and sometimes he doesn't take too kindly to

anyone pointing out deficiencies in his organisation, but that is a personal thing. But I do admire him because he was the driving force behind it along with a guy called **Don Robinson** who is a man I have a great affection for because he was a real showman.

He held a *Radio 270* night out in Leeds which was an all nighter, top of the bill was The Who and people like Pinkertons Assorted Colours; he had a barbecue, a fairground, all under cover in what had been the old tram sheds, and is now a big exhibition centre, and **Jimmy Savile** riding in on an elephant. It was a memorable night and in fact heavily features in a film I am involved in.

Fan magazines that reported the 'fun life' of the shipboard DJ's were in some respects accurate. Boredom was relieved with practical jokes that more often than not caused havoc:

"The Dutch crew, and they actually wore clogs, big hulking Dutch guys and one of them was at the mast, it wasn't one of the DJs it was one of the radio technicians a scouse, Mike I think. He saw these clogs lying on the deck and got these 6″ nails and hammered them to the deck and this guy shimmied down the mast and put his feet into them and tried to walk. It backfired and he sprained his ankle very badly and was taken off. But the upshot of this was that for two weeks this guy lived in terror because the Dutchman never said anything, he knew who had done it. By two weeks he thought it had been forgotten, but on Saturday we used to have a saloon where we all shared a long table with a hatch just above the table and there was a wrench on the table which this Dutchman had left there. We were having our lunch and Mike was in the middle and the Dutchman shouts 'Mike, the wrench', and Mike hands him the wrench to find this ape like hand grabbing his wrist. I was next to him and he just shot out through the hole in the roof and seconds later there was this plop as he hit the ocean. In one swoop pulled him out into the ocean, and that was his revenge, it was full of stuff like that because boredom takes a terrible toll and it is where you get the mischief and silliness.

There was one guy who was a pompous asshole and nobody could stand him and we finally decided we had had enough of it. So we got this cylinder type vacuum cleaner, rigged behind the microphone just before his show, packed it full of self raising flour from the galley. The switch was in another studio, so all we had to do was throw the switch and it was on blow; he started his show and we threw the switch, all crammed into the other studio, and nothing happened. All you could hear was this 'zzzzz', it was the power building up behind this flour, we had packed it in too tight. He heard it and said 'I don't know if you can hear that noise, it is probably some technical fault, we'll sort that out, but right now . . .' and suddenly the whole window went white and it was like a roaring sound on the air and him coughing and spluttering and we just panicked and rushed into the saloon and sat down innocently. Seconds later we heard a jingle and he came in covered in powder and one of the Australian guys who was working with us looked up and said 'I didn't know you were

into flower power'; it threw the whole place apart.

Like so many of the early jocks Paul Burnett graduated to *Radio Luxembourg*, which still enjoyed its reputation as a leading music station. Surprisingly this was due to the intervention of one of the most experienced and professional of DJ's around, Pete Murray, to whom Paul is understandably grateful:

"New guys come along and at the time I was one of those new guys. I was working for *Manx Radio* and **Pete Murray** came over, like I do now, in fact I met somebody who told me they had got a job on radio through something I had done for them, which reminded me of what Pete had done for me.

Really I interviewed him for the station, we got on really well, he is a very nice man, we ended up chatting about this and that and he said what do you hope to do and I said I would love to work with the big station, *208* was as magic as BBC. He said he happened to know that they have somebody who they are not too happy with and are looking for a replacement, I shall mention your name, if you'd like. And you think that is very nice — I only found out years later, I didn't know that he had, because I sent a tape in anyway and got a letter back saying they'd like to see me.

I got the job on *Luxembourg* and a couple of years later I found out from **Geoffrey Everitt** who was the boss man of *Luxembourg*, he told me Pete had said keep an eye open for this young lad who will be writing in.

I really appreciate that, it is really nice because a year after I joined *Radio Luxembourg* I was doing a show with Pete called the Peter and Paul show sponsored by Clarks Shoes, pretending I was in Luxembourg.

Although we couldn't technically do it, we sat opposite each other, him asking me how the weather was in Luxembourg and me asking how the weather was in London. Then I managed to stay at his place, he was living with **Valerie Singleton** then and he must have realised I was ga-ga. I was really in awe, he was one of the big four: **Pete Murray, David Jacobs, Jimmy Savile** and **Alan Freeman**, the only DJs prior to pirate radio. People forget about that, radio in the early 60s was two hours of pop a day if you were lucky."

The perils of working for a foreign based station came home to Burnett when the regular flight he caught to Luxembourg was involved in an infamous crash at Staines:

"A friend of mine in Manchester arranged some gigs for me, I was the first one on *Luxembourg* to start doing PAs on a regular basis on my night off. Saturday morning I would fly over, and get the gigs, by the time you had paid you air fare you would end up with pennies but it was great and also a contact, you feel very remote when you are living in a foreign country.

I did that every fortnight. I had been over the week before and I used to get the five o'clock flight to Brussels and catch the connection to Luxembourg on a Sunday evening in

LIFE AFLOAT

Life aboard "OCEAAN 7" is different yes—but all the mod-cons and comforts of home keep the 270 men happy in their two weeks stint. Just take a look at a typical lunch prepared by the 270 chef:

Choice of Fruit Juices. Mushroom or Onion Soup. Roast Lamb or Chicken (with baked potatoes and vegetables). Apple Crois-sant with cream or ice cream. Tea/coffee.

Understandably, no signs of malnutrition on board. In their spare time the boys have a choice of a wide variety of activities. They sleep, fish, sleep, weather permitting they swim, sunbathe or sleep. They play darts, hand-ball, deck tennis—or read and watch television. Answering fan-mail is one big time-consuming task for the d.j.'s.

A daily tender vessel from Scarborough keeps the boys in touch with the world outside, bringing out books, magazines, newspapers, per-sonal mail and, of course, supplies and provisions for 270

RADIO 270

the North's first commercial radio. Heard it yet? It's not just a station, it's a sensation. All over the North, and Midlands and even overseas—it's hit them in Holland like a hole in the sea wall.

And it's GOT SOMETHING FOR EVERYONE. Up to the minute news bulletins and weather reports, competi-tions, sports reports and more music, more often.

Tune in now to 18½ hours a day—6.30 a.m. to 1 a.m.—throughout the industrial North and Midlands, serving an audience of 15 million.

Apply now for a rate card and full particulars of our advertising terms. You'll be surprised how little it costs to increase your business turnover. Others have proved the success of RADIO 270 advertising—why not you?

Are you arranging a special function? Barbecue? Swinging Beat Party? Dinner Dance? Then advertise your special "Date" on RADIO 270 at very little cost with big results. Don't delay—write or phone today: RADIO 270, ADVERTISING SALES, ALBEMARLE CHAMBERS, ALBEMARLE CRESCENT, SCARBOROUGH.

Phone: Scarborough 63645.

SOMEBODY'S IDEA OF A 'FUN' PROSPECTUS FOR YORKSHIRE'S FAVOURITE RADIO STATION

time for my show at 11 o'clock.

The following weekend I sat in a car with my wife and the five o'clock flight out of Heathrow had crashed, I can even remember the name of the crew: Captain Keyes and co-pilot Keighley, but I was on that plane the week before and the week after. It is a bit frightening. **Bob Stewart** had an even worse one, he actually had a ticket in his hand for a seat on the jumbo that crashed out of Paris. He was coming to England on a big DC 10 and he had a ticket that he only changed because he managed to get a direct flight. That makes you a bit nervous but, after you do it every week, it doesn't bother me at all now."

The English crew of the Luxembourg station

reacted to the problems of being in a foreign land in different ways. Quite a few found it oppressive whilst others relied on the practical jokes that had made life on board ship so bearable:

"You put your finger on it with the name **Tony Prince**. I shall always be grateful to Tony. I have a love hate relation-ship with Tony, most people do. If you live with him he can get right up your nose, because he is a real extrovert, an over the top character and he will do things you'd like to do but don't have the balls for and of course you all end up in the shit.

It was never boring when Tony was there and it can be boring and I know that after our time when it was. **Kid Jensen** Tony Prince, **Mark Wesley** and myself were together for five years and they were great years for me. It could be very boring but Prince made it so it wasn't boring.

The station had kind of lost some of its momentum because people had put up with the bad reception because there was nothing else, even when *Radio 1* was in full swing it went off the air at seven in the evening.

Then along came the commercial stations and it is not really the station it was. You felt important, to me it was just as good as *Radio 1*. I realise it wasn't now, but it is prestigious, and it got your name known; it takes a couple of years of regular broadcasting before your name means anything. The route to *Radio 1* was via *Radio Luxembourg:* **Kid Jensen**, **Mike Read**, **Peter Powell**, and myself.''

The decisions on board the pirate ships were in the hands of the management who were, after all, interested primarily in turning a profit on the original investment. The DJ's then, as now, had little to do with policy making:

''No it was management and I think it (policy) was in terms of the ship instead of individual jocks. It takes longer than the time we had — *Radio 270* was on the air only 18 months, but it seemed to have a great impact in the shops and the areas around for advertising.

We were told to keep the chat to a minimum, just keep the music going, that is what made us different from the Light Programme, it is pathetic, it is no secret to the BBC that *Radio 1* exists because it is the only thing they could think of . . .

I think pirate broadcasting appeals to me at times because I listen to lots of *Laser* and I like the way the guys and girls are; it is a young mans job to live with that, if you have a family you can't go back, I wouldn't like to go back to it.

Caroline. . . after the bill people wanted to turn their attention elsewhere, *Radio 1* was where it was at, there was no real necessity for it. I never felt the same about post Bill pirate radio, anybody worth their salt wasn't working for the pirates afterwards.''

Although it was viewed by the public as an arbitary crushing, the Marine Offences Act was greeted by the shipboard broadcasters with mixed feelings. Very few felt that the 'job' should entail breaking the law in reality, despite the colourful pirate tag, although there was a sadness that the party was over:

''We all did, but it also had a certain respectability before the Bill went through — that you are a pirate but you weren't breaking any laws, the law didn't exist to break.

It is a personal thing, I just didn't feel the same about *Caroline* after the Bill as I did before, it was a businesslike operation and I have got no time for people who don't regard it on a businesslike level because I think there is a certain integrity there. You give people what they want, that is a business edict, you are not out there to play your own choice of music or to be on a personal ego trip.

I was always very for the play list, I like the play list, it took it out of my hands. I can play the music I like at home. It sounds odd, obviously I want to play the music I like on the air but if it doesn't match up with what people are buying, who am I to say that they are wrong.''

But even on *270* the business ethic and the playlist was a predominent factor. Whilst the public at large seemingly enjoyed a spontaneous output of hits the music was strictly controlled behind the scenes:

''You could play what you liked within the play list, the format that **Blackburn** uses on *Radio London* although he restricts it to a junk/funk rhythm/blues sort of thing. But ours was just based on the chart, the top 40 and then the ones bubbling under and 20 golden oldies. So you had your list within that 100 records, I could leave out the **Ken Dodd** if it didn't meet with my taste, I stuck to my own personal thing and that was fair enough, there were always guys ready to play Ken Dodd.

When you choose the new records, I ended up actually doing the play list, so that was a great ego thing. I could do my bit for educating the public saying this is what they should be hearing, the public can only judge by what they hear on the radio, what they are going to go out and buy. Having said that I don't see why I should, but that is what you are paid to do.''

The older generation soundly dismissed the pirate ships as 'floating juke boxes', a not wholly inaccurate description shared by most of the BBC producers:

''That is what the accusation by the older generation was, but they didn't realise that was what people wanted from pirate radio.

I was eight years with *Radio 1* and that was a result of the crash course. It was dead easy to get a job on pirate radio, anybody who had the bottle for a start or had done some hospital radio, could get on pirate radio. Keeping your job was the thing, people came and went very quickly, for every guy who made it there would be 100 who wouldn't.

I don't want to talk about pirate radio as though it was a golden era of broadcasting, some of the broadcasters were bloody awful because they were amateur. Me too, I listen to some of my old tapes and could cringe, but I was learning on the job and at its best it was fabulous but at its worst it was bloody awful. People even loved the awful part of it, listen to *Laser* now. When I like *Laser* is when they are not being super professional — two guys the other night were on and they had been watching the TV that evening, and they both started singing the theme from Star Trek and they had me in stitches; off the head, funny, spontaneous and what pirate radio should be about is spontaneity, human beings talking to human beings with nothing inbetween and hopefully we will get back to that.''

PAUL BURNETT: WORKING ON A FILM BASED ON *RADIO 270*

DAVE CASH

VARIOUS (CANADA/USA)
RADIO LONDON
BBC LIGHT PROGRAMME

RADIO ONE
RADIO MONTE CARLO
CAPITAL RADIO

On the wall of Dave Cash's London flat, just around the corner from *Capital Radio* **is a small framed photograph given to him by a friend. It shows the** *MV Galaxy* **half submerged in some harbour, some place. It is a telling and poignant reminder of just how long ago it was that the** *Galaxy* **housed** *Radio London,* **the blockbuster of pirate radio operations in the 1960s. Cash was involved in radio before he ever set foot on a pirate station, properly trained in Canada as a result of his unofficial dual nationality:**

"I got into radio in Vancouver, British Columbia in '63, with training and all that garbage they used to do, started making the tea and ended up doing midnight to dawn.

I came to England in December '64, Christmas Eve, and had just about had enough of America, I had been around America on a sabbatical just doing radio where and when I could which wasn't very often; I heard from a friend of mine over here about the pirates and thought I would come and investigate.

The one thing I didn't like about American radio was the fact that the real talent of the radio had disappeared with the advent of the disc jockey. I lived in England for a good part of my childhood, born in Edgware, my dad didn't fancy post-war Britain and we went to Canada in '47 where he got a better job because they were much more advanced in his field. I came back to England when I was 11 to go to school and went back to Canada when I was 16, so I had a good chunk of my childhood here.

I went to school over here so got to learn both cultures. When I got back to Canada **Freiberg** and people like that were still making it but what had happened was the disc jockey had taken over, it was just play this, play that, play the music. I always felt that was a bit of a waste. Well **Reith** had said 'we're going to educate the people' and we said 'why not just talk to them and get them involved' because, with the advent of television, radio had to go somewhere; the BBC didn't want to know and we didn't want American type radio here. So the guys that gathered in '64 for the pirates were really disenchanted with American radio and wouldn't be allowed at the BBC because they didn't wear a dinner jacket.

There was a producer called **Wifred D'eath** and he was very pro-pirates and he was the one **Kenny Everett** sent a tape to, so that sort of thing. There were people within the Corporation but the management didn't want to know, so when the pirates started we just grabbed it as an opportunity to do the type of broadcasting we wanted to do."

Dave Cash's introduction to the pirate ships was, once again, that stroke of good fortune quickly becoming a familiar pattern amongst recruits to the fledgling radio business . . .
"I was walking down Curzon Street and when I came to it . . . I knew one guy here a guy called **Billy Street**. He had just married **Norma** and she was pregnant with the first of their five children and he said 'come on over and stay with me and see what happens'. So I came with enough bread for one good night in the Washington Hotel in Curzon Street and was walking up to meet Billy who was working in Berkeley Square as an Insurance Agent. As I passed 17 Curzon Street, there was a great booming familiar Texan voice and I went in and it was **Ben Tony**, who I had met in Dallas when I had done my round trip. He said, 'nobody out there knows what the fuck is going on, it sounds like a pile of crap'.

My name was **Dave Wish** then, and he said 'meet **Tony Windsor** out there, he knows what he is doing', and listening to it, it really sounded weird.

Pete Brady joined Tony Windsor who was brilliant and still is, the doyen of our group of people, a very honest man. One thing in the radio business, a lot of the time, is that the management are really not concerned about what is going on the radio.

Phil Birch was the Managing guy and Ben Tony was the programme controller, a huge man from Texas, and then Windsor was the head jock. He was a good 15 to 20 years older than the rest of us and had 10 years experience in Australia, so he knew what was happening and he just moulded this team together.

In the beginning there was Brady and Kenny and myself and a guy called **Dave Dennis** who is now **Neil Spence** and works for National Broadcasting. I still keep in touch with him. **Earl Richmond** who disappeared from the scene some years ago and is living in Bangkok I

believe and **Duncan Johnson**, that was the team as I can remember.

If you actually stop to think about the reality of it, you would never go out there. It was absolute hell to live, really, because you were on a converted mine sweeper, the cabins after the first year got better, but it was not comfortable by any stretch of the imagination. That was when the weather was good, when the weather was bad . . . My Lord.

Cash, like Emperor Rosko, had some experience of the sea and so the actual life aboard was understandable, if not bearable. It still had its moments of real risk and danger, not least when trying to leave . . .
"Sure I was a good sailor, I had been at naval college anyway and I loved being on the sea, but if you are in a storm at sea you have to move. If you can move you can go into it and feel you are beating it, but we were anchored. At the back, the studios were in the stern, you went up and down; imagine a 20' wave, whatever the mathematics of it is you are bucking 30/40'. It is just like being tethered, which you are, in the studio and the back the ship is going up and down.

You are in the studio and you can't play any records you have to play tapes, there was padding all the way round, because there were bulkheads they had to pad them because people could get hurt, the ship could come down and meet your head.

Sometimes we used to go a month before the tug could get alongside, you were nearly killed getting on and off that boat. You could go off in a Force 6, but the tender that used to take us on and off was Dutch and it was a trawler, it could handle rough seas; but if it came along your stern — both ships rocking about — you just had to jump as the tender was coming down. If you jumped when it was coming up you splattered all over the deck . . ."

It was on the shore leave that the jocks got some idea of the impact that their music and personalities were making on the young public. It was a sensation that bonded them to their near neighbours in the North Sea, on board *Radio Caroline.*
"I think there was friendly competition between *London* and *Caroline* so we knew the *Caroline* boys and we looked on it that as long as one of us was in the business . . . They were slightly different, more English than us, we were more Americanised and we had all the fancy jingles and that stuff. We were also copied by *Radio England,* they were like *Laser* is now — just a jukebox.

We had a slightly different presentation, both were equally valid, and when we came ashore, at first there wasn't too much hassle but after about a year it just made you feel great. We stuck together basically and we just used to go mad.

It was rock'n roll on the road. In the 60s rock'n roll

on the road was the thing. I actually did a show with Kenny, we had the Kenny and Cash Show; we did a thing called the Steam Packet — we did three dates in East Anglia and some other people did the rest of the country. We did East Anglia and one in London. Steam Packet was headed by **Julie Driscoll** and **Brian Auger, Long John Baldry**, bringing up the rear was **Rod Stewart** and playing piano for Baldry was **Elton John, (Reggie Dwight)**.

The Steam Packet was *the* show and it was Brian Auger's Trinity, Rod wasn't with the Faces then but, God, he was a good singer, he was absolutely superb. He was the best rock'n roll blues singer we ever had and the one thing about that period I will never forget was being able to be there when that went on. Because all the stuff that has happened recently is nothing like it used to be then . . . "

With the boom in DJ's as personalities running parallel to the fantastic, exploding, music business; the scene quickly came to equal money — and lots of it. Pirate broadcasting began to reap similar rewards and its practitioners began to re-evalute their own positions . . .

" . . . that was our roots and it was great to experience it. Long John Baldry had the most brilliant voice and so did Julie Driscoll, Brian Auger was just a maniac, so that is what we used to do when we were ashore. We used to do things like The Walker Brothers tour, we did more than just discos, because we used to use the tours for interviews.

I think it was something that people had not experienced before in that it wasn't the type of DJs that had been. There was **Alan Freeman**, he had come from Australia; **Pete Murray**, I always thought was great; and **David Jacobs**, because David was so much a gentleman. They had personalities and **Brian Matthews** of course, probably the best DJ of that era, superb voice and timing and everything, probably the best.

Most of the people who worked for the BBC were just 'this is the light programme, it is ten past twelve, I don't have a name or a face', that was the idea of the dinner jackets for the 6 o'clock news.

What we did was just say 'Hello, you alright then' which has finally come down today to 'Hello John got a new motor' . . .

The Marine Offences Act appeared all to quickly on the horizon, Dave Cash toyed with the idea of sticking it out in the North Sea and defying the law:

"I contemplated it definitely, but during the time the first reading failed, then it had its second reading and succeeded, you had to see the writing on the wall even though it failed in the time. The thought was that we were professionals, we were in the business because we wanted to make a career out of it, whether to be journalists or disc

M.V. GALAXY, HOME OF *RADIO LONDON*

jockeys or both. It was our business, our work, so we could rebel and stay there but most of us thought it was kind of a waste of time. If you are really outlawed then fine, **Johnnie Walker** did it, he was the symbol and where is he now, *Wiltshire Radio* back at ILR. He stuck it out, somebody had to, so did **Robby Dale** who now is in the cleaning business and doing extremely well."

Cash left to join the BBC ahead of the MOA rush, at the same time he kept up his interest in unorthadox broadcasting by doing a stint with *Radio Monte Carlo*, news in the pirate radio world because they hired their transmitters after hours to the hip *Radio Geronimo*, a short lived effort that collapsed through lack of money.

"After *Radio 1,2,3* and *4*, after the change over I did a thing called Monday Monday, again the Beeb employed a lot of us which was great because we had a job. I think a lot of Beeb people thought we would just set into their mould and become BBC people; well we didn't, or most of us didn't, plus the fact that we brought people out of the Beeb who would have gone that way, people like **David Symonds** who was a Beeb boy through and through but was one of us so therefore carried on. **Keith Skues**, what a man, I think Keith was on a pirate at first, I can't remember, then he went to the Beeb, but he never changed . . . and **John Peel** of course.

So I started on the Light Programme with Monday Monday and also Midday Spin on Thursday. I have actually got my first billing in the Radio Times which says 'Dave Cash presents an hour and a half of recorded music'.

I worked for *Radio 1* for a couple of years, four years I guess, the only show I have ever lost in my life, actually saying 'we're taking you off because we have got somebody else to fill the slot', was to **Terry Wogan** and he was always good. Then I did a series of programmes for them, because the Beeb look after you very well. As much as they are arty in a lot of ways they are great at organisation and they let me do a couple of Country shows and a series of chat shows on *Radio 4,* which I thoroughly enjoyed. Then I had a chance to work for *Monte Carlo;* a guy called **Maurice** got hold of me and said 'do you want to come and live and work in Monte Carlo'.

We worked out at the *Monte Carlo* studios in Monte Carlo and did the show with Kenny and **Tommy Vance**. Tommy and I had to begin with an hour and a half a night each of really painful stuff.

Some shows came from here — London, we used to do our committment in London because I was working for the Beeb doing some Country shows as well, and you would wind up your committments for three or four weeks then piss off to Monte Carlo, Sunshine Studios.

We stayed down for a while and worked and for a while it was absolute heaven."

Cash admits that the sojourn to Monte Carlo and the station there does not compare with the activites of the pirate stations. It was not a similar concept, but it goes to illustrate that he was flexible enough to look at any broadcast form that happened along, a factor not so common amongst the older BBC employees.

"I don't think *Monte Carlo* was a concept in broadcasting at all, it was a service for English speaking people in the South of France basically and also hopefully coming into London, where it never really made much impact.

A very large radio complex, broadcasting in maybe five or six languages at different times of the day. The Stones were thinking of going down there and spending some time in the South of France and it was thought it would be a good thing to have an English speaking, albeit late night, radio station in the South of France.

We were part of Monte Carlo, not pirates at all. But there was no concept, it was just a great time, it made up for the other five years at the Beeb, also a marriage that blew up."

Cash's appreciation of the past is tempered with the experiences of broadcasting he had previously, and many since. It was the type of presentation, he feels, that made the real impact, not the location onboard ship . . .

"You never know there is history in the making, what you hope is you will succeed in what you are trying to do and

So what would happen... you would get a sort of BBC Home, Light and Third and then you'd get a programme *Monday Monday* with me doing it

We had **Jimi Hendrix** on and this mad producer **Keith Bates**, he was one of the best balancers the BBC had in those days and when The Beatles used to come down and do live stuff they would ask for Bates.

So typical BBC, they made him a producer, he was too good as an engineer, so they made him a producer; but he was mad. I said 'why don't we book Jimi Hendrix' and he said 'yes, let's do it', so we had Hendrix live. All these little old ladies would come in to do their knitting at one o'clock because it was a live show with **Ray McVae** and the Band of the Day. The singer with Ray McVae was a guy who has just had a hit: **Joe Fagin**; and **Patsy Jones**, so we used to get them doing covers of the old songs. You have never lived until you have heard Ray McVae do A Whiter Shade of Pale, it is absolutely hysterical.

He is a good lad and a good band but it wasn't rock'n roll. So Hendrix would come on as a guest, we had a guest every week, most of the time it would be **Vince Hill**. Hendrix starts playing 'Hey Joe' and picking his guitar with his teeth and all these old ladies in the front row are having a haemorrhage 'I can't believe it, this is the BBC', there are lots of crazy stories like that.

Then *1,2,3* and *4* happened and we all moved, I did the afternoon show for two years.

Kenny 'n' Cash for breakfast

CAPITAL RADIO
in tune with London
539m Medium Wave – 95·8 VHF Stereo

CAPITAL RADIO PUBLICITY BLURB FOR THE DYNAMIC DUO

CASH AT HOME IN LONDON

get through to people.

I don't think the pirate side of it is the concept, it just happened to be pirate. The concept of broadcasting was to talk to people on a one to one basis which some people do and always have done extremely well. I find on television **Whicker** does it very well, **Alastair Cook** is superb and **David Attenborough**, a lot of people... **Johnny Morris** in his way does it.

What we wanted to do — we thought it was a waste of air time for disc jockeys to sit there like they do in the States and blabber, you may as well get a computer to do it. We thought that it would be nice to get people together and have a good time and at the same time help the community as a whole if you can, that is why Capital Help Line was set up, because if you give something to people, like anything they give back...

"I think *Caroline* is a bit of a lost dream, it is full of bravado, but doesn't really prove anything anymore. It did then, it is like **Ali** going back in the ring that one too many times and pirate radio now has got something to say land-based.

Laser is very popular at the moment because it just plays so much good music all the time, it is a jukebox. There is a place for a jukebox within the scheme of things, there is a place for all types of broadcasting, but our type of broadcasting was not that.

It made its statement in the 60s and now it is not worth recapturing that statement or trying to. I think the people enjoy the pirates and I think the land based pirates have something to say, I always thought *DBC* was great because it just showed that culture, brought it to the surface and I think that radio, especially, television is too orientated, but radio could bring these cultures to the surface and let other people understand them a lot better.

If you listen to *DBC, Jackie* or some of the South London stuff, *Horizon* and stations like that, you can cop into things happening in South London and you know what they are talking about."

Cash is a partner in a successful TV production company and one of their projects is to present the pirate radio phenomena with more accent on the political connotations. Additionally Cash and his colleagues have produced pilots for a superb music series provisionally titled *Buzz*, which, if the they are anything to go by, will soon be a boss showcase televisual event.

"I think a lot of people have done a lot of things on the pirates and a lot of people have lived through them and a lot of stories haven't been told because it is political, so we are going to tackle that end of it.

We were very lucky because we put *Buzz* together over about two months with **Phil Bishop** directing and we learned a lot from him, a lot about editing and **Alastair**, my partner in the production company has been in the business 15 years. He left it about five years ago and started what he calls an ordinary business and did very well — about £5/6 milllion turnover a year. He is a musician, writes and performs and so on, so it is a good little combination and the other thing that I wanted to do was to move into... not the more serious side of things because that is not my bag, but if the telly work is there... I just want to create a new slot for telly of doing 'people' stories really.

I did a show for HTV for two years, eleven years ago, which was called the Dave Cash Radio Programme on television, a day in the life of a disc jockey really. I wrote and performed in that and I had to play a part in that not myself, but a part written for me and I enjoyed it. But it just got me used to television so I can work with a TV camera but the type of things we hope to be getting into in the next few years can't be explained because it is in my head and not on paper."

Dave Cash repects the past and what the pirate radio ships and their following did for his career. But the photograph of the half sunk *Galaxy* on his wall does not cloud his professional judgement of the current radio climate or developments within the industry...

"Go back? No, I don't think so; it would be like **Ali** going back into the ring that extra time, I wouldn't put myself through that. When I was 21 I had the youth and the stamina to go through it, now I am 42 and there are other things that I do, I just don't think one should try and recapture youth, you have to look forward to something that you might be able to do in the next 10 or 15 years.

I am quite happy on radio, I love working on radio and as long as I know the radio game, you are only as successful as your last set of figures and my last set of figures was good, so I am happy with it and if they ever die a death I'll end up doing McDonalds voice-overs or something..."

PIRATE RADIO

RADIO ESSEX IS MY STATION 24 HOURS A DAY 222 METRES

1965

A year of minor setbacks for **RADIO VERONICA**. The ship breaks anchor and nearly runs aground. Back at the land based studios, a large construction programme on the opposite side of the street stops all recording until the early hours of the morning.

JAN 13/14 Severe gales wrench off the starboard anchor from **CAROLINE** and she begins to drift. Within days a new 1½ ton anchor is fitted and 4½ tons of cable. The Isle of Man tourist board is given free advertising and the ship becomes a local attraction.

JAN 22 Britain, Belgium, Denmark, France, Greece, Luxembourg and Sweden sign a Council of Europe Agreement to ban pirate radio broadcasts 'on board ships, aircraft or any other floating or airborne objects'. The agreement bans not only the broadcasts themselves but also bans anyone from providing the stations with supplies, equipment or broadcasting material.

JAN 24 David Block, publicity executive with

CAROLINE says the agreement may force them to stop for a short while, but they will still be able to carry on by getting supplies from countries who are not signatories to it, such as Spain or Holland. They plan to change their land based headquarters to New York. **David Block** says 'we are putting up a fight because we feel the British people are on our side'.

FEB Reg Calvert plans another station, this time on **Knock John Sands**, a nearby fort. It has been earmarked by **Roy Bates** for his new station, and for a while there exists a state of virtual warfare between the two stations.
At **Roy Bates'** home in Southend, his wife says: 'My husband's been working hard on this project and I know damn well he won't just give it up.'

FEB 24 Walton-on-the-Naze lifeboat is called to attend a sick DJ on board **RADIO LONDON**, who has gastric flu.

FEB The success of **CAROLINE, LONDON** and others

prompts The National Broadcasting Development Committee headed by **Sir Harmar Nicholls MP,** (and including **Lords Mancroft,** and **Grantchester** and the historian **A.J.P. Taylor** on its committee) to press for Government action to start commercial radio.
RADIO CAROLINE: present advertisement revenue runs at £15,000 weekly according to a spokesman.

MARCH 2 After negotiations with the owners of **RADIO INVICTA** a group of Kent businessmen, including **Charles Evans** and **David Lye**, begin to refit the station in order to improve its output. They spend about £7,000 on new equipment. Test transmissions start, identified as **RADIO KING**.
MARCH 3 In the House of Commons **Mr Benn** asks '. . really what are pirates but hulks with big masts, carrying microphones, gramaphones and seasick disc jockeys. Anybody who thinks that by mooring **RADIO LONDON** in a berth in Barking you have pioneered local radio had better have another think'

MARCH 21 RADIO INVICTA, after many rumours of takover attempts (including one involving The Batchelors), finally closes

MARCH 22 The Post-Master General, **Mr. Benn**, says that he has evidence to show that pirate ships have interfered with communications between ships and the shore on at least sixteen occasions in the previous year.

MARCH 24 KING RADIO formerly **RADIO INVICTA** begins transmissions on 237 and 238 meters. There staple diet is very middle-of-the-road, and consequently they fail to attract a wide audience — about 20,000 at most.

APR 23 The chief engineer on **RADIO LONDON** is taken to Colchester Hospital seriously ill.

MAY 13 RADIO PAMELA begins test transmissions. The station is aboard a boat off Clacton, broadcasting on 1343 kHz (233 meters).

JUNE Twenty seven **RADIO SYD** advertisers face court hearings. Meanwhile on **Cheeta II** plans are being made for TV transmissions. $US. 40,000 is invested in equipping the ship and $US. 150,000 on studio installations including a 30 meter antenna.

JUNE 7 Continuing problems on **KING RADIO** prompt its

RIGHT: A TRENDY GROUP OF TOP *LONDON* DJ'S — RECOGNISE ANY?

LISTEN TO GOOD MUSIC K-I-N-G RADIO On 236 METRES Medium Wave Band

52

owners to call in **Ted Allebeury.** A new Company Estuary Radio Ltd is set up to acquire control of the station. The company spends thousands in persuading the Kent businessmen involved to relinquish control and to begin a refit of the station.

JULY 10 Estuary Radio Ltd submits a formal application for a licence to broadcast — it is refused.

AUG 20 Captain **W. Bundega**, of RADIO LONDON is rushed to hospital in Clacton, with appendicitis.

SEPT 22 KING RADIO previously **Pepper's** RADIO INVICTA closes and RADIO 390 opens in it's place. The old station stays on the air for a few days to urges its listeners to turn in to the new frequency. The new station has had in all some £150,000 spent on it. A new 297 foot mast has been constructed on one of the towers, two new studios have been built.

SEPT 25 RADIO 390 begins regular broadcasts. It immediately attracts a regular audience. Its signal is remarkably clear, and its output is light middle-of-the-road. It covers most of England, and broadcasts from 6.30am to midnight.
On an interview with the News of the World RADIO 390 manager **Ted Allebeury** describes his formula for daytime radio: to attract the housewives during the day: 'we talk rather softly, rather intimately to them. We try to be as cosy as a pair of old slippers. We behave as they'd like their husbands to behave. We just keep them company until he gets home at night.'

OCT Negotiations commence between RADIO CAROLINE and RADIO CITY for CAROLINE to take over CITY. Some promo material is broadcast by CAROLINE from Shivering Sands.

OCT 25 First test transmissions begin for RADIO ESSEX. This new station is owned by **Roy Bates**, a former fisherman.

NOV 7 RADIO ESSEX on Knock John Fort, begins transmitting. Its formula is to prove successful. Middle-of-the-road during the day and moving into the Top 40 in the evening. At this time, too, a group of businessmen, in the North of England, form a limited company, Ellambar Investments Ltd. The leader of the group is **Wilf Proudfoot**. They announce the intention of setting up an offshore commercial station for the North of England.

DEC Ronan O'Rahilly comments on the progress of CAROLINE and his role in it: 'The Irish breed rebels where the English gentlemen. The English like to watch the action, the Irish provide it.'

Sweden: **Britt Wadner** is given a three month jail sentence whilst test television transmissions on UHF, channel E41, emanate from Cheeta II. On her release she is met by affluent looking businessmen creating rumours that she represents a secret, larger organisation. Rumours in the business claim things are not 100% well with RADIO SYD.

DEC 8 The Postmaster General **Mr Benn** tells the House of Commons that legislation to deal with the pirates outside territorial waters was being prepared and would be introduced 'as soon as is practicable'.
At a press conference in the evening he says that he hopes his announcement will be taken as a warning, which will be acted upon by the pirates. 'I do not think these are desparate criminals. The forts are aware of the position — this is a reminder. They can rest assured that if we get evidence that they are infringing the **Wireless Telegraphy Acts**, we will prosecute', he says. He states further that there is no

chance of these stations being given a licence. 'The future does not exist for them' he declares.

DEC 10 RADIO **390** begins a campaign to get its listeners to write to **Mr Benn** to say they support the station. Several hundred people write, only a few say they support the Government stand.

DEC 16 Because of the volume of mail he has received **Mr Benn** decides to answer the people who have written to him: and explain why he is attempting to stop the pirates. 'Naturally the pirate stations themselves won't give you the reasons why. So perhaps I can do so. The unhappy fact is that the pirate stations have simply taken over wavelengths that belong to other countries. These wavelengths were divided up between the countries of Europe by international agreement, an agreement to which Britain pledged its word. In disregard of this agreement, the pirates are causing serious interference with the enjoyment of people on the continent who now find they cannot hear their own local stations clearly.'

DEC 18 RADIO CAROLINE holds its first 'Pop Ball' in Liverpool.
Figures published show that RADIO CAROLINE is getting about £30,000 a month, but with two ships to run it leaves very little room for profit. Meanwhile RADIO LONDON is reputed to be earning about £60,000 per month.

DEC 19 Despite the Postmaster Generals' announcement of further legislation against pirate radio, a 500 ton former lightship The Comet prepares for transmission on

LOOK AT THEM ALL — THEY'RE HAVIN' A BALL!

Thousands of Radio Scotland 242 Clan members and their guests packed the Locarno Ballroom, Glasgow, for the first-ever 242 Clan Ball. In a sensational night of entertainment and sparkling music, they heard the Over-landers, Beat-stalkers, Moon-rakers, Poets, Meridians, and Habits. All the deejays were there (except old Ugly Bob Spencer out there on the boat) for an evening that really swung.

Poetic—

Radio Scotland deejay Paul Young and fans.

RADIO SCOTLAND
SWINGS TO YOU ON **242** METRES

New Years Eve as RADIO SCOTLAND.

he is returned to Holland.

DEC 24 The police of Harwich get a call from RADIO LONDON to say that a man is running amok aboard the vessel with a knife. They come to the ship and take him off. As he is a Dutch national,

DEC 31 RADIO SCOTLAND begins transmission on 1241 kHz (242 meters). Over the next few weeks it will test on several different frequencies. Its call sign is 'Swinging to you on 242'.

LOTS OF 'FUN' AT A *RADIO SCOTLAND* CLAN NIGHT OUT SWINGIN'...?

ns having a ball.

A night to remember for thousands of Clan members like

or—he's lovely!! Who's lovely? They're all lovely if they're Poets.

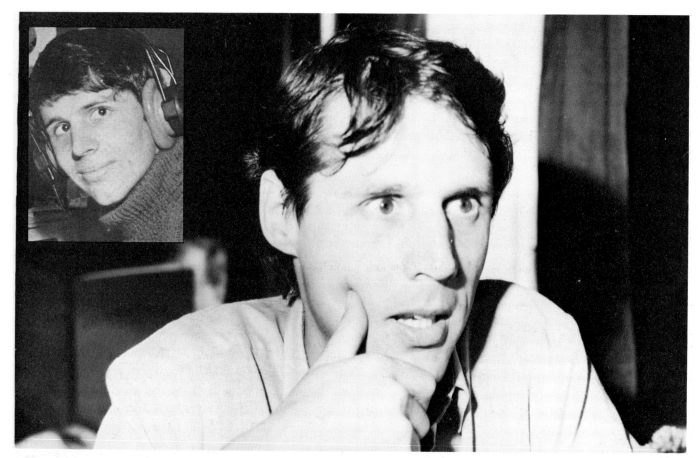

MARK WESLEY

RADIO ESSEX
RADIO 270
RADIO SCOTLAND

RADIO NORDZEE INTERNATIONAL
LUXEMBOURG
SAXON RADIO (ILR)

Mark Wesley's career has a curious after image because for a time he worked as Mark West, a fact which confused some chroniclers of the offshore radio business. In his time Wesley/West has worked the whole gamut of radio stations — from the most primitive Thames Fort to the international station in the Grand Duchy of Luxembourg. Wesley is a natural raconteur and librarian — he has on video a transcription from a Super 8 film he took of his first days on the *Radio Essex* fort, surely priceless footage today. His introduction to broadcasting was in line with the spirit of the times — pure luck:

"I'm as common as muck, standard education, from Essex, down by the creek. I was born in water never to leave water,

that is why I moved inland, I wash but other than that. . .

I left school when I was 15, I had hoped I might get into animation, this is a lesser known Wesley, it is one of those pipe dreams. I didn't want to be in front, I wanted to be one of the people behind the curtains.

I also was a musician and I think I still am, I was in a group, a R'n R band and the Manager we had was a guy that had worked on a pirate station and he found himself the manager of a cinema, the Kingsway Cinema. His name was **Rusty (Vince) Hammer**.

Pirate radio stations had only been on the air for about six months and it fascinated me the way it fascinated everybody else, but like everybody else you think it's a job for other people, another persons type of job, you don't even think about it. I was happy to be a musician, and I hoped that our band would be successful, we were selling records. I used to talk an awful lot about pirate radio and what it was like and more and more of this was getting to me and I was thinking this is something very special.

I worked putting new carpets in cars and re – lining seats and God knows what else, I was an apprentice. But at lunch time I used to go and see the Manager in the cinema which was just down the road from where I worked, it was a cinema but they were only doing wrestling on a Friday and Sunday, we used to kick a football around in the foyer and talk about setting up our own radio station.

We said it was possible, we said 'there are other forts out there and if we could get hold of a transmitter, turntables and generator, we could get out and start a radio station'. My thought was if we have got the goods, we can play our records on the radio, we could promote our own records. I was 17 and it didn't occur to me to see the practical side of it.

I thought my dad knows all about transmitters, I'll get him to make one. Vince decided he would go along to the various coastal areas and find a fisherman willing to take us out to one of the forts to have a look and see which one we should claim. He came back one day and said 'I've met this bloke who has a small fishing boat, and his boss owns a whole load, but he said he can't let me use the boat until I speak to this chap and this was **Roy Bates**'.

He said 'I met **Roy Bates**, and spoke to him and he said it's funny you should say that because I am doing exactly the same thing, I plan to start a radio station and I have my eye on a particular fort'.

I think he had already been on a fort, so it started off at that point. Having invited Vince to become the Programme Director, and yours truly to become the first disc jockey.

That sounds unfair, but it is one of those curious quirks, I had no right to become the first disc jockey but that kind of invitation to join might have happened to a lot of other people in different ways. Anyway I was the first disc jockey.

We had a bit of trouble with a radio station who claimed our fort and they tried to set up, they didn't attempt to stop us but they went to some lengths to stop us getting a generator on board and a transmitter. We went out in a party and we turfed them off and sent them back to *Radio City*. That is how a mythology about Roy Bates and how he was a real pirate started.

I think we got painted pretty black by other radio crews from that moment onwards. We used their generator until we got the old generators going, a chap called **Richard Palmer** who is still in the engineering business now. I think we gave *City* back their generator, I'm not sure, but we finally got on the air and did these test transmissions.''

The forts that stood around the Thames Estuary had been built by both the Navy and Army to protect the sea lanes and were of various shape and design. Logically they had seemed to be more suitable for a radio base than a ship, but as they survived into the sixties their condition had deteriorated:

''It wasn't radio, it was an outward bound course and 'by the way you are on the air in a minute'.

It could have been considerably better, given enough money the ideal situation was a stable platform on the sea bed, 12 miles off Canvey Island in our case. We had all kinds of problems. Our first advertiser was Channel Airways. I remember the first words I ever uttered on the air which were the test transmissions, it was 'this is *Radio Essex* the voice of Essex on 222 meters and this is test transmission'. Then I got them to embellish it by saying 'this is Phase 1 of our test transmission', because we never seemed to get off test transmission for one reason or another. I said 'we should change this and make it sound like we are doing something, let's call it Phase 1 and next week we can call it Phase 2', but nothing was done to make it any different.

The problems of cleaning the place up and making it habitable were phenomenal, imagine a fort such as it was, on two columns, metal, steel, iron platform, caked with rust, sitting on concrete columns in which were eight floors, some of them under the water. About 80ft up. I was a 17 year old and it was great, if it happened now I would think twice. I've a lovely film of those times, I've got it on video actually, I filmed it on 8mm.

It would be very easy for me to say 'what a lot of crap', because it couldn't have any real bearing on the furtherance of the broadcasting idea, but what it did for me was got me on that rung, the first rung of the ladder, it was a rusty ladder.''

Fisherman Bates was one of the entrepreneurs who were regarded with veiled suspicion by observers of the booming radio business, although it could not be denied that Bates and his ilk threw themselves into the off shore broadcast arena very energetically:

''He had ideas of expanding as well, he wanted to get *Radio Kent* organised and there was another similar shaped fort off of Margate — I think it is called the *Tongue Sands Fort*, but it had been wrecked. That didn't stop Bates, there were two concrete columns and the whole thing had been hit, there was a hole in one of the legs so it was full of water and apart from that the platform had shifted about six feet and you were in this really deep water, the shipping channel, some 12 miles out. In a far more dangerous position, and all we had in the way of an transmitter at that time was a communication link with *Radio Essex*.

One day a storm brewed up and the other leg started to fill with water and it was panic stations, God bless Bates he did come out and rescue us, so we lived to see another day, I'm not sure what happened to the fort, I don't think it fell over, if we had stayed on the platform we would have been o.k.

On *Radio Essex* we used the night time transmitter, when we weren't on the air officially broadcasting. We would finish at 10 o'clock at night, later we did go 24 hours but in the early days we closed down, it might have been about 12 o'clock. We had no other communication other than the transmitter, so we had to close down then put our shopping list through. There were times when we got very, very, desparate, you could be on the thing for 10 weeks and that is a long time.''

Wesley's transfer from the rigours of an Essex Fort also meant the move to a ship. *Radio 270* **was anchored off Scarborough in North Yorkshire, a popular station in the** *Caroline* **mould:**
"Rusty left for *270* and offered his services to them, so too did a couple of guys, one voice you will hear a lot on television, a guy called **Roger Scott** (not of *Capital Radio*), **Greg Banks** as he was known. He was on *Essex* with me, and so too was **Jerry Zeeler** who has subsequently gone on to manage radio stations. Those chaps were invited over by **Vince** and later on I was invited over to replace **Paul** who was leaving.

I was there about three months, I must say that it was an interesting ship. I liked the one week on and one week off, you can imagine after my period with *Radio Essex* of 10 weeks at a stretch, suddenly one week on, one week off — this was a holiday, but I didn't realise how seasick I was going to get. The ship I found rocked a lot.

What was curious about it was the fact that it used to dock at Bridlington, it was the only pirate radio ship that actually used to go inland. We would finish transmissions at whatever high tide at night was convenient, about 10 o'clock or 12 o'clock, and shove into Bridlington Harbour. There the village policeman would come and give us a mug of coffee and a request, and then we would leave on the next high tide about 3 o'clock in the morning or 6,7,8 o'clock to get the first part of our breakfast show out.

We looked forward to those moments because it was our one respite from the appalling cooking by this chap, some Yorkshire seaman, who was the worst cook I have ever met, worse than my mother. What would happen, the ship would be moored in Bridlington Harbour and if it was morning we would go down to the cafe and have our breakfast and go back to the ship with him moaning 'I've got your breakfast ready', and we would say 'I'm not really very hungry at the moment.'

It didn't matter, because there was no Marine Offences Act at that time, as long as we weren't transmitting, it was illegal to use that equipment within the three mile limit of British territorial waters, so we switched off, chugged inside the three mile limit.''

Mark Wesley, or West as he was at this time, then moved rapidly onwards to Scotland and joined with the *Comet* **and Tommy Shields'** *Radio Scotland.*
"I had the syndrome that you find most younger broadcasters have and that is the nomad syndrome, they wander around, like the grass is greener everywhere but where they are.

They seem to take the attitude that if this radio station will employ them it can't be very good, or you can look at it that way, and I had that attitude as well. I didn't think much of the radio station that is true, I thought they were skinflints,

RADIO ESSEX ATOP THE FORT ON SHIVERING SANDS

and I felt we had no respect from the management, like: 'disc jockeys — they get in the way of making the profit'.

I did what so many people were doing at the time, you saw an opportunity to get onto another radio station, it started to become a thing where you could say how many radio stations you had been on. It wasn't the real criteria for moving on it was just that you got fed up with the conditions that you were lumbered with. You would always try to cut back so that the profit could be more, if they could make a profit at all, which I suspect they must have done.

Put yourself in my position. I was on *270* and I was able to hear Scotland all the way down there, a big powerful transmitter, that had some kind of association in the first days with *Radio London* or something. I'm not sure, but there was some kind of connection. It had a bit of magic although I knew nothing else about it. I just wrote and sent a demo tape and they wrote back and sent me some tickets; which was either that or **Wilf Proudfoot** was giving me the tickets. But I went up there and went on board this ship which was further out than any ship I had ever been on, the Firth of Forth was in the deepest water, it stunk of diesel, I couldn't pronounce any names...

There were two 10Kw transmitters on board, it was quite an operation really, and I can't see any reason why it could have failed, but I don't think it did as well as it should have done. I think it was badly managed, but it should have done well.''

MARK WESLEY AND SHIPMATE ABOARD THE OCEAAN 7, ANCHORED OFF SCARBOROUGH

Tommy Shields called it a day when the Marine Offences Act came into being, although he had begun to cause political ripples before that with his campaign to legitimise the station. It had, however, suffered numerous breaks in transmission and re-locations at the end . . .

"Yes, *Scotland* closed down and I was on the last transmission. I took the attitude that I'm sure a lot of other people took that if the Government it going to take my job away from me they can bloody well pay for it until I find another job, so I went on the dole.

Do you know I don't remember that there was any payola on *270* or *Scotland*. There may have been the odd one record or two but I really don't remember.

I'm sure certain records came out, if we got every record, that was another thing, half the radio stations I was on you were bloody lucky if they sent all the records.

On *270* there was a card, you just ticked off the records you played so the guy following you wouldn't play the same records. On *Radio Scotland* I really believe you just played, what the hell, if there is anything find it and play it.

It was all discs on the ship although what happened **Stuart Henry** couldn't manage it so he sent tapes, when I was out there he wasn't sending tapes out although he did a special as I recall towards the end, I think it may have been on the last day, I can't remember.

I was there relatively quite early in the game, but I would have thought people whose names inevitably appear all the time are those who appear on the most popular of them all, which would have been *Caroline* and *Radio London* and I must admit the one thing I would have loved to have done was worked on *Caroline* or *London*."

MARK WESLEY IN THE STUDIO, *RADIO NORDZEE INTERNATIONAL*

Wesley didn't find himself at a loose end for very long and after a time as a record plugger projecting such artists as The Beatles and Elton John he developed his own music and started playing dates. The next broadcast job Mark did was aboard the infamous *Radio Nordsee International***, a situation that arose out of the blue . . .**

"We had a contract with **Shapiro Bernstein** publishing and a record deal with CBS and the first thing we ever recorded we got **Andrew Lloyd Webber** into arrange; this is before Joseph and his Technicolour Dreamcoat or whatever it was called . . . the publishing company said 'we've got this chap called Andrew Lloyd Webber', and I had never heard of him. But to be honest I never heard of anybody else either and I said 'let's have a listen, what has he done', they played me this and I said 'sounds like he knows how to arrange'.

The fact is that *Nordzee* was a radio station run by a couple of guys trying to make a killing in pirate radio. I don't know whether they were idealists, define an idealist; an idealist is a person who seizes and goes for it, and in that case I understand they made their money selling arms to Biafra or something. They made a lot of money in their connections with Biafra, that is what I have heard. These are rumours I'm repeating, and they invested an awful lot of that money in it setting up, before I joined, **Andy Archer** had already been

on board. I had a phone call.

I was in a different group, and we had made a couple more records, more flops incidentally, and I was getting fed up with paying HP on a Marshall amplifier system and push starting Trojan vans. We did regular spots at the Whisky-A-Go-Go and we always had to park the van downhill so it would start when we left.

I was really cheesed off thinking that there must be more to life than this, and out of the blue I got a phone call from **Roger Day.** At the time he was running it and he said to me 'are you interested in working out here', I don't think I had met him before, maybe occasionally and I said I think I might be interested. He told me what the salary was, which was very good, two weeks on and two weeks off and he said 'if you are interested, meet me at Gatwick Airport tomorrow morning at 8 o'clock', and I said 'I think I might be able to find myself there'. I didn't even take the guys address, I just packed my bags and drove up to Gatwick."

Mark Wesley was on board the *Mebo 11* **on the fateful misty morning when Kees Manders tried to cut the anchor chain and pirate the pirate. The incident didn't seem so sinister in retrospect although the sensation of seeing the Dutch Royal Navy answer the cries for help broadcast over the air he remembers well. However, despite suc-**

cesses with Elton John's records, Wesley eventually moved onto *Radio Luxembourg,* **still regarded as a major station at that time:**

"For me it was very much the high point in my career as a broadcaster, no doubt it was halcyon days for *Radio Luxembourg* and very much so for me as well. We were hanging onto the coat tails of the stars of the day, we had a magazine FAB 208, which at that time was incredibly successful, it was selling in many hundreds of thousands on a weekly basis. They were showing pictures of the stars and they were making stars and we were playing their music and I feel very sure that we were a very important part of peoples lives at that time. It certainly showed in the amount of gigs I was doing, the discos and the reaction we had, it was absolutely incredible.

It was absolutely marvellous. I don't say that I necessarily enjoyed it, the money was o.k. and I must admit there was an ego thing there as well. But eventually it did start to pass and it somehow or other came in round about the same time as local radio, commercial radio, *Radio 1* was o.k. but *Radio 1* at the time wasn't providing really a pop night time service, so we worked very closely with Radio 1 in many respects.

However local commercial radio comes along and a nice clear signal and a lot of them are doing music at night, and I think eventually it started to whittle away to what was a very small audience anyway.

THE ARTIST AS SAILOR

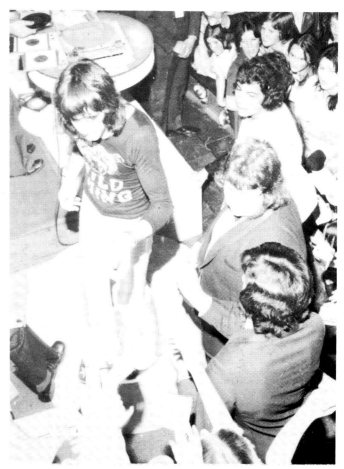

THE REALITY OF THE ROADSHOW, WESLEY DIRECTS

After 11 years there was no doubt that it was time to move on, I tried for *Radio 1* and it wasn't forthcoming. I heard stories from friends of mine that they had been told that my career as a plugger went against me at *Radio 1* which was rather a shame, that being the case there is not much I can do about it. I can't change the pattern, and those that knew me from then are still operating now for *Radio 1* and nothing is going to change.

I take a very practical view of these things and I knew there was no way I could stay, I have to move. You could easily retire at *Luxembourg*, you can go on forever, so I had to get back to Britain and try and start something else, again in radio if I can. It's a good way of making money and maybe get back into my music which hovered in the background, because while I was with *Radio Luxembourg* a number of records I had released got into the top five in New York and Los Angeles *Billboard* charts."

In fact, for all his modesty, Wesley is an accomplished musician and his own business making musical links and jingles is becoming more and more successful. So much so that he is thinking of giving himself over to it on a full time basis . . .

"I play a number of instruments, I'm what you might call a

multi-instrumentalist: spoons, washboard, string bass, and I kind of sing of sorts, but I also produce. I had a interesting contract with EMI Records to produce for them, I had a number of song writing contracts with publishing houses, a lot of production work, big production, good fun, I really enjoyed it and I am beginning to get back into that.

This opportunity to get back into that music has arisen because I have returned to Britain and am working in local radio. On *Luxembourg* there is a style and that is the style they employ you for and it is a very narrow style with no chance of embellishing to broaden it, but a good opportunity to stagnate and so I was stagnating and I had been for some years; so I just had to get back to Britain.

I came to *Radio Orwell, Saxon Radio* was part of *Radio Orwell* as an overall company called *Suffolk Radio* and I moved to *Saxon* to do their breakfast show. Buying a house and setting up my own studio, which is what I am doing. I have got a 24 track studio, and I write music logos for advertisers on television and radio and that is beginning to take a very important part of my life.

I don't want to be a performing musician, I enjoy being backstage, this is why I have never really tried to get into television, apart from the obvious — I'd look damn stupid on telly. But apart from that I don't have the confidence to do it, it worries me, it scares me. I am very happy to be behind, I like to be part of things but not visibly part.

It's image creation, look at **Kenny Everett** he is not the most good looking guy you'll ever see in the world, but for what he does it really doesn't matter. What he has are great character images, ideas. Now I don't have that ability and I think the most important part of a persons career is what they can and what they can't do."

Mark Wesley is cautious about the state of broadcasting in the present day, whilst acknowledging the past he is aware that time has passed since the days of *Radio Essex*. It's a view shared by most of the more experienced DJs that originated from those halcyon days of 1964:
"I think **Ronan** is making a fool of himself, I think whatever campaign he thinks he is on is nothing to do with radio.

Everybody is listening to *Laser* and it is very popular and for very good reasons. They are doing what *Caroline* should have done, and I don't know whether it is immediately apparent to you but to me, you have a brand new audience, a brand new younger audience who haven't heard these wonderful stories of life on board ship and salty radio and all the rest of it. *Caroline* came on the air trying to ignore that and missed the boat. Whilst *Laser* have come on and they employ people that have never really experienced in their own life pirate radio; so they have youth; but the enthusiasm of 'Christ we are at sea, isn't it a wonderful thing' and that enthusiasm comes across and with popular music it is a winning formula."

RADIO NORDZEE INTERNATIONAL

MARK WESLEY AS LUXEMBOURG HEART-THROB

The local radio outfits, with their strict observations of IBA dictates come in for a lot of criticism and it is surprising the number of ex-pirate DJs that eventually join these stations. Mark Wesley feels that even these local operations are trying their best to move with the flow, even if it is only by hiring the right personnel:

"The thing that may surprise you about commercial radio and it certainly surprised me, I've learned a lot of lessons... I had an opinion formed by conversations with other people, a totally false impression really of what commercial radio was supposed to be about — that is it is full of worthy items and worthy people saying worthy things which are absolutely worthless. As far as a viable commercial operation is concerned (and they are commercial operations when it gets down to the bottom line), the important thing is the figure at the end of the financial year, does it pay the wages? does it pay a dividend?

It is a business and unfortunately because so many of the local stations have actually broadcast to the IBA and not their listeners in an attempt to cling to their franchise and they have in many respects written their own death warrant.

What the listeners want and what the IBA want are often two different things, as a matter of fact the IBA might share that opinion because there is a different attitude towards commercial radio in Britain now even by the IBA.

There are certain fundamental areas of decency and propriety, things which are proper, which they don't want the commercial stations to go beyond. But there is an enormous change, certainly amongst the radio stations that I am on now.

In a way it's capital E for Entertainment, cut down all the words, we've done our bit and where necessary we'll stick it in, but other than that what we are going for are the listeners. We want to entertain and if we can't make it our listeners retaliate, we don't need the IBA to tell us we are not doing the job properly and in many respects that is true of a lot of radio stations. Although of course we have to very careful as they are still our lord and masters."

The local radio stations are eager to play the ratings game and are quick to pick up on any broadcasting system that increases the listening figures. The importance of the current offshore stations have yet to demonstrate the part they are playing in this, but the illegal stations land-based in the big cities are causing programme directors a lot of concern, if not the advertising executives. Dublin's *Radio Nova* is already the boss Irish station after a relatively short life — with advertising and 61% of listening cake to prove it.

"The show that I run at the moment started off as you might expect as a worthy programme. In fact it's taken a totally different view now because I am encouraged to do more of my *Radio Luxembourg* style than I would ever have guessed and I am enjoying very much. I enjoyed what I was doing in the past, but I am doing a lot of work on a weekly basis on the programme, there is a lot of newspaper contribution to the programme, it is a very newsy breakfast programme. There is a lot of music, it's fast, snappy, whimsical, humourous I like to think. It has a journalistic element but not of a very serious nature really, it's opinions and comment."

Mark Wesley's days aboard the pirate ships stay with him in one respect because, although he has disposed of Mark West, his broadcast name from the past stays with him, as it does with many of his old radio shipmates...

"This is the truth — My name is Martin Wesley Goble, that is my full family name, and Goble is not a very good broadcasting name, so we avoided that. Wesley I didn't think too much about it, but when I was doing the test transmissions on *Radio Essex* I had to come up with some kind of a name and it was not uncommon, in fact it was the thing to do to come up with a kind of stage name.

Martin always struck me as being a weak forename that didn't really have any ring to it. Wesley, well, most people who know me as Martin call me Mart but you can't cut Wesley down to Wes, so we changed it slightly to **Mark West**.

That is what happened there on *270*, I was **Mark West** but later on during my days as a writer, after the Government had closed us down, I was talking to a publishing chap and he said 'Wesley is a terrific name you should use it, it is unusual enough to be worth using' so I thought it was maybe right. I knew I wouldn't waste very much by dropping West because nobody knows the name West anyway, so it was really a twin career..."

The Sound of the Nation!
Radio Ca

1966

JAN 11 A force 8 gale caused the **Galaxy**, **RADIO LONDON**, to drag anchor.

JAN 12 2.45am. Clacton lifeboat is launched as the **Galaxy** had begun to drift and ends up close to Clacton. It is within territorial limits, so is off the air, until it is tugged back. In a typical touch of humour, the first record it plays when it re-appears is The Beatles 'Day Tripper'.

JAN 18 At Wimbledon magistrates Court **Martin McDonald** an 18 year old student at Kingston Technical College, is found guilty of broadcasting without a licence. He is fined £2, and his transmitter is ordered to be confiscated.
For the previous six months he had been transmitting from his home in Wimbledon, **RADIO SHAMELESS**, broadcasting music and commercials for Kingston Rag Week.

JAN 20 **Cheeta II** has to move because of thick pack ice and broadcasting stops. Instead of returning to her position she sails for England.

JAN 20 Force eight blowing when **CAROLINE SOUTH** closes down at 8pm. The anchor chain breaks around 10.30pm and the **Mi Amigo** drifts. Walton coastguard tries to warn the ship to no avail. Walton lifeboat is delayed by the weather for an hour, the **Kent** sets out from Felixstowe and **Offshore One** sets off for the stricken vessel. The supply tender reaches **Mi Amigo** just as she is about to go around.
12.20am: **Mi Amigo** aground at Frinton-on-Sea, a miraculous beaching avoiding concrete groynes all up the coastline.

JAN 21 The Walton Life Saving Apparatus Company rig up a breechers bouy and help **CAROLINE SOUTH** staff ashore. Rescued this way are **Tom Lodge, Tony Blackburn, DLT, Norman St. John** and **Graham Webb** along with engineering staff.

JAN 22 **Mi Amigo's** captain, using a technique known as kedging, refloats the radio ship.

JAN 23 **Mi Amigo** arrives in Zaandam, after being assisted by escort tug **Titan**, to inspect any damage from the beaching at Frinton.

JAN 31 **Cheeta II** arrives off Harwich on loan to **Ronan O'Rahilly** while **Mi Amigo** is in dry dock

FEB 10 **RADIO SCOTLAND** runs into trouble in heavy seas, and the pump on board is unable to cope with the five feet of water in her chain locker.

FEB 10 The Ministry of Defence says that it considered that attempting to remove **RADIO 390** and **RADIO CITY** from disused army forts in the Thames estuary would prove 'so hazardous as to make it not a viable proposition at the moment'. A spokesman also questioned the use of the word

'trespassers' to describe the stations due to the uncertainty over who now owns the land.

FEB 16 **RADIO LONDON** announces that it will now pay composers a share of its advertising revenue. It will pay 1.6 of its revenue to the

oline

389 ENGLISH SERVICE METRES
259 DUTCH SERVICE METRES

Performing Rights Society.

FEB 26 The former Dutch fishing vessel **Oceaan VII** arrives in Scarborough to be fitted out as a radio ship. The opening date for **RADIO 270** is announced to be 1st April.

FEB 27 6am: **Mi Amigo**

CAROLINE JOCKS 'RELAXING AND HAVING FUN'

takes over sole broadcasting for **CAROLINE SOUTH**

APR 2 A day after the intended opening of **RADIO 270** it is still not heard. In the morning a force 7 gale

causes havoc to the mast.

APR 5 **Mi Amigo** with a new 50kw transmitter leaves Zaandam for Frinton. Test transmissions begin two weeks later on 256 meters (1169kHz)

APR 15 According to a survey carried out by National Opinion Polls Ltd., on the listening habits of young adults, **RADIO LONDON** leads the field with 8,390,000 listeners, **RADIO CAROLINE** has 6,270,000, **RADIO 390** has 1,700,000 and **RADIO SCOTLAND** has 2,450,000. The survey was carried out in February and involved 2,465 interviews.

APR 18 After a fault on the aerial, broadcasts from the Mi Amigo cease. **Tony Blackburn** becomes forever a hero by climbing up the mast and effecting a repair.

APR 22 The Comet is towed from its location off Dunbar to five miles off Troon. This is done to improve reception in the West of Scotland. Unfortunately the spot they chose is inside territorial waters.

APR 25 Effectively there are two **CAROLINE SOUTH** stations **Cheeta II** and **Mi Amigo**. Shows feature a talk between the two ships.

MAY 1 **Cheeta II** ceases to relay **CAROLINE SOUTH** transmissions

MAY 3 First test transmissions begin for **BRITAIN RADIO** on 1320kHz (227m). Tests also begin for **RADIO ENGLAND** on 845 kHz (355 meters), but changes after protest from Italy to 1320 kHz (227 meters). Both these stations are aboard the motor vessel **Olga Patricia**, a 167 foot landing craft. It has been re-fitted in Key Biscayne, Miami and brought to a position three miles off Walton-on-the-Naze.

MAY **RADIO LONDON** undergoes a refit — the aim to increase its output to some 75 Kw. Altogether about £50,000 is spent on refurbishment.

A press release announces that a new station is to come on air in August from the coast of Essex. Its purpose is: ' to broadcast unfettered, without fear or favour, political thought on a wide range of subjects to the British Isles.'

MAY 23 A series of disasters strike **The Comet**: a fire destroys one of the generators on the ship, then a storm blows up and damages the aerial and finally they lose the ships lifeboat.

355 BRITAIN RA

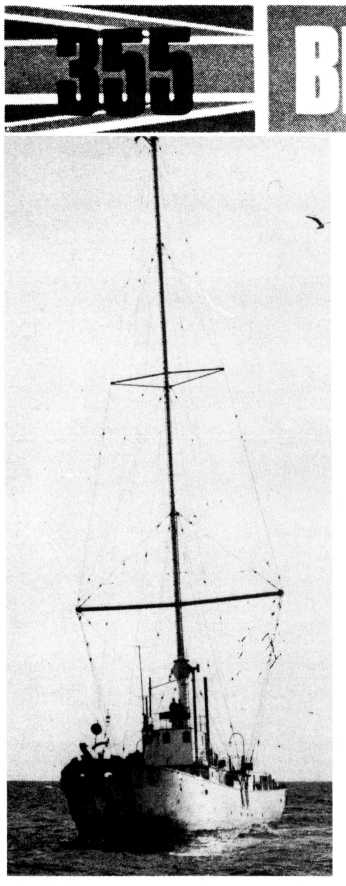

RADIO VERONICA drops half hourly programmes in favour of two hourly ones. **Borkum Riff** is put out to grass and the station continues on a new vessel, the **Norderney**. The **Norderney** has a better aeriel rig and a more powerful transmitter (10Kw).

JUN 3 The Italian government complains that transmissions from **BRITAIN RADIO** are interfering with **RADIO ROMA II**, so it changes to 845 kHz (355 meters).

JUN 4 First transmissions from **RADIO 270** on 1115 kHz (269 meters) with 10Kw of power. The station is to go off the air several times because of technical problems.

JUN 16 News breaks that **RADIO LONDON** is interested in buying **RADIO CITY**. With a view to this **Duncan Johnson** and **Keith Skues** from **LONDON** motor down with **Reg Calvert** to inspect the fort. What they see does not impress them.

JUN 18 'Swinging' **RADIO ENGLAND** starts transmission.

The style is very American, non-stop music, very different from the other stations. It does not appeal to British tastes.

JUN 19 Walton lifeboat rescues two men adrift in a lifeboat from **Cheeta II** anchored off Frinton. Regular transmissions start from **RADIO BRITAIN**. The station is launched with a party for 600 guests at the Hilton.

JUN 20 Major **Oliver Smedley**, head of the former **RADIO ATLANTA** boards **RADIO CITY** with a group of ten workman and takes re-possession of a 10kw transmitter which he had delivered to **RADIO CITY** but which had not been paid for. He leaves, but the other men stay aboard the fort. **RADIO CITY** stays off the air.

JUN 21 **Reg Calvert** calls on **Oliver Smedley** at his home in Saffron Walden in Essex. **Reg Calvert** is shot dead.

JUN 22 Police visit Shivering Sands questioning

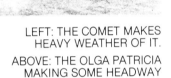

LEFT: THE COMET MAKES
HEAVY WEATHER OF IT.
ABOVE: THE OLGA PATRICIA
MAKING SOME HEADWAY

the raiding party and the crew.

JUN 24 With the help of spare crystals for the transmitter, **RADIO CITY** restarts. **Reg Calvert's** wife, **Dorothy** assumes control of the station.

JUL 2 The Government publishes **The Marine etc., Broadcasting (Offences) Bill**, under which broadcasts from ships and marine structures will be unlawful. It will be unlawful to instigate, finance, provide goods or in any way aid a pirate radio. The maximum penalties are to be two years imprisonment, or a fine, or both.

JUL 3 The BBC announces that it has made a proposal to the Post Office 'on the question of providing a continuous entertainment programme', probably to be carried on the Light Programme medium

wavelength (247 meters).

Bad weather along the North East coast forces **RADIO 270** off the air. The aerial is damaged in the high winds.

JUL 8 An oil fired boiler in the living quarters at **Shivering Sands** explodes, and for a while **RADIO CITY** comes off the air while the blaze is brought under control.

JUL 18 Major **Oliver Smedley,** at Saffron Walden, is charged with murder, but the charge is reduced to one of manslaughter. He is to appear before Chelmsford Assizes in October. Bail is granted in the sum of £500 with two sureties of £500 each.

JUL 21 Cheeta II breaks her anchor and seriously undermanned, has to accept a tow from the tug **Agama**, who moors her near the Harkstead Buoy.

JUL 22 Oceaan VII enters Bridlington for supplies and repairs.
Customs men and an Admiralty Marshal nail a writ to the mast of **Cheeta II**. The tow company claim salvage for the rescue.

SEPT 21 David Lye, as Secretary of Estuary Radio Ltd. is served with three summonses for illegal broadcasting.

SEPT 28 Roy Bates is served a summons alleging contravention of the 1949 Wireless Telegraphy Act. He

insists that he will fight. He also announces an improvement in the tranmitters for **RADIO ESSEX** and that with these refurbishments the station will adapt a new name: **BBMS (BRITAINS BETTER MUSIC STATION).**

SEPT 29 M.M.McLaren, a Rate payers candidate in the

local elections for Harwich Town Council puts an advertisement about his campaign on **BRITAIN RADIO**. He wins by about 250 votes, despite the dubious legality of his actions.

SEPT Captain **Martin Gips** of the **CAROLINE** marries DJ **Mick Luvzit** (sic) and **Janet Teret** by his authority as Master of a Panamanian vessel.

OCT 11 The trial opens at Chelmsford Assizes of Major **Oliver Smedley**. He is charged with the manslaughter of **Reginald Calvert**. Without retiring, the jury decide on a verdict of 'Not Guilty'.

OCT 28 Drama surrounds the Oceaan VII with the **RADIO 270** DJs being unaware of it: a letter is delivered to the station saying a limpet mine had been attached to the ship. As the ship did not keep a regular radio watch, it could not be contacted. It is late in the afternoon before the ship is roused. A search ensues, but nothing is found. Rough seas prevent a complete inspection.

OCT 31 After normal close down at 8.30pm **RADIO CAROLINE NORTH** comes back on air at 10.30 pm to test transmit on 257 meters (1169 kHz). These tests continued every night until November 24. Day time output remains on 197 meters (1520 kHz).

NOV 4 RADIO ENGLAND closes down and is replaced by the Dutch station, **RADIO DOLFIJN**, popularly known as **RADIO FLIPPER**, and later **RADIO 227**.

NOV 16 4pm: Cheeta II is released from arrest after **Mr Justice Brandon** rejects a request for her sale. At the hearing another owner, one of a number, appears — U.B.A. Establishment of Lichtenstein.

NOV 24 Sir Peter Rawlinson QC acting on behalf of Estuary Radio Ltd argues in Longport Magistrates Court, Canterbury that the **Red Sands Towers** are eight and a half miles from land, and were therefore outside territorial waters.

NOV 26 Estuary Radio is found guilty and fined £100. **Ted Allebeury** , as Managing Director, and **David Lye** as Secretary are given absolute discharges. The prosecution are refused leave to confiscate equipment. 11 pm a message is broadcast explaining the days events. This is followed by 'On a Clear Day' the stations signature tune and the station closes with the National Anthem.

NOV 30 Roy Bates is before Rochford Magistrates Court, defending himself against charges of illegal broadcasting. His argument is that **Knock John** is in international waters. This could be proved by the fact that continental fisherman had used these waters for years without anyone trying to prevent them.

This is rejected, and he is given one week to pay the £100 fine.

DEC 2 'This is **RADIO HAURAKI** the station for young New Zealanders, broadcasting test transmissions from the **Tiri** in the Hauraki Gulf'.

This bland announcement hides a tale of high drama which begins with the purchase of a 90 foot long wooden ship **Tiri** by **David**

Gapes and others to break the broadcasting monopoly of the New Zealand Broadcasting Corporation. At this point the New Zealand Government intervenes and orders the **Tiri** to be detained for 'safety reasons'.' Eventually the **Tiri** attempts to sail, but is detained. The courts dismiss the charges, and the **Tiri** sets off to its position in the Colville

Channel, North Island, New Zealand. The whole affiar has assured enormous interest, and the station opens in a blaze of publicity.

DEC 12 In the High Court, before the Lord Chief Justice, **Lord Parker, Lord Justice Salmon** and **Mr. Justice Blane, Sir Peter Rawlinson QC** argues against the conviction of Estuary Radio

Ltd, still basing his argument on the question of the territorial limit.

DEC 13 Judgement is given against Estuary Radio by a two to one verdict, **Lord Justice Salmon** being in favour of the defendants. Although the station is given leave to appeal to the House of Lords the directors reluctantly decide against it on the grounds of cost.

DEC 18 All future transmissions from **RADIO CAROLINE NORTH** are issued on 257 meters (1169 kHz)

DEC 19 **RADIO 390** returns to the air, five weeks after losing a court case in Canterbury, Kent for illegal broadcasting. **Mr Ted Allebeury** the station director says he has evidence to show that his station, at **Red Sands Tower** in the Thames Estuary, is outside the territorial limit.

ABOVE: THE MI AMIGO AT ANCHOR (INSET) THE CREW AND DJS ON BOARD LEFT: THE TIRI TRYING TO REFLOAT

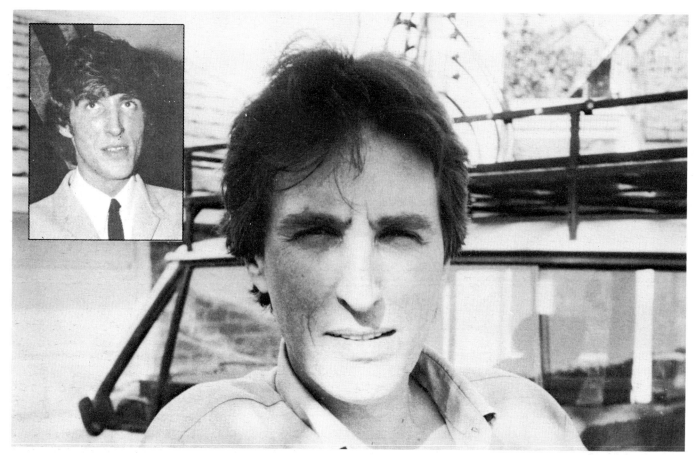

JOHNNIE WALKER

RADIO ENGLAND
CAROLINE SOUTH
RADIO ONE

VARIOUS (USA)
LUXEMBOURG
WILTSHIRE RADIO (ILR)

Johnnie Walker has always been regarded as the idealist amongst the original pirate radio men — he was one of those who stayed on board when the MOA sent his colleagues home, and he still feels that the arbitrary closing of the free radios was a crime in itself. Walker's start in the communications business was surprisingly similar to other pirate jocks:

"I left school at 16, I failed all my 'O' levels and the headmaster wrote home, it was a private school, and suggested to my father that he was wasting his money investing any more in his son's education as I was basically unacademic; which in my terms means I was just a rebel and couldn't accept that what they considered was so dreadfully important, actually was.

I left at 16, went to Gloucester and became a car mechanic and I started doing DJ work in the evening. I went to this pub on the outskirts of Birmingham and really, after having been told by my parents to 'turn the volume down', it was one of the first discotheques and heard really loud for the first time and thought, somehow or other I'm going to be involved with this in my life. So I pestered the Manager of the *Locarno Ballroom* in Birmingham every week for about four months and told him what a great DJ I was and how stupid he was not to hire me on the spot and eventually he got so fed up with me nagging him he said 'alright, start next week then'.

Being that I was working this premier nightspot in Birmingham, — the *Mecca Locarno Ballroom* which was the biggest in the country, I could then go to other clubs in the Birmingham area, and say 'I'm the Locarno DJ, you should hire me on the nights that I'm not working there'. So eventually I was working six nights week as a DJ until one and two in the morning then trying to be awake and together at 9am to flog motor cars. I had just passed my 21st birthday and that was a watershed in my life, I looked out the car showroom window and thought 'My God, there is all this big wide world outside and if I don't make a move now I could be sitting in this seat 20 or 30 years on'. So I told the Manager I was going to be a DJ, he said 'leave now, you don't need to work a week's notice', so I walked home. My parents went absolutely nuts that I had thrown away this secure future. The next day the Daily Mirror ran an article on *Radio England,* this was '65 so *Caroline* and *London* were already on the air and I used to listen to them a lot. 'Pirates' was a great name for them whatever anybody might say; they were illegal, irreverent, they were free, it appealed to everything in me.

So I rang the Daily Mirror on the Monday, found out where the advance party for *Radio England* was located, which was the Hilton Hotel, rang them up and they said 'send us an audition tape'. Instead of posting it, I took it down on the train the next day and knocked on the door and spoke to them and I think they were impressed by my initiative in travelling down so I was hired. So I was out of work in fact for one day, which was just the most immense piece of luck and it is strange the way these things come about because I would never have applied for that job had it not been for a member of the audience in a discotheque on Saturday night, when the article appeared, who came up to me and said 'did you read about this new station in the Daily Mirror, you should have a go at that'. So some anonymous bloke somewhere is to blame for all of it."

I started with *Radio England* in May '66, that was a very troubled station, with a lack of organisation and a very bad signal. When the opportunity to move to *Caroline* in October '66 I leapt at it, started with the station filling in for the DJ's who were away on their weeks leave and eventually got the nine to midnight show."

The problems with money and ownership on this station signified to some the entrance of unscrupulous interests into what was generally regarded as a peace and love business:
"It was run by two Americans **Bill Vick** and **Don Pearson.** They were supposedly both extremely wealthy. One was an oil millionaire, who very much looked the part, with ten gallon hat and cowboy boots, JR, and everything. But I am not sure. I think it was maybe all pretty much of a scam."

Two separate stations operated from the same boat, the *Laissez Faire*, anchored off Walton on the Naze. Walker remembers the opulence of the launch party . . .
"*Britain Radio* was good music MOR and *Radio England* was pop. But they stayed at the Hilton Hotel for about three months, they held an amazing party which cost £10,000 which in those days was a lot of money. Then I think they both disappeared, they did a moonlight back to the States without pay-

ing the Hilton Hotel a penny, so I rather think the whole thing was a bit of a scam.

It plodded on but I think *Radio England* with a Dutch format and *Britain Radio* continued. I can't remember what happened actually, but it eventually went off the air."

The importance of the Peir-Vick experience for Johnnie Walker was the valuable introduction to that 'first lady' of broadcasting, the *Caroline*, the ship that embodied all he felt about the rebel radio concept
"*Caroline* had the name although *Radio London* had tended to steal a large part of the pirate audience because when it arrived it was the first one with a 50,000 watt transmitter and *Caroline* was still only on about 10,000 watts.

Radio London had a much more professional approach and format, style and jingles and all the rest of it, so *Caroline* was knocked sideways a bit by the arrival of *Radio London*. But to me *London* was like a radio station that happened to be on a boat in the sea, *Radio Caroline* was a pirate station, first and foremost. It did crazy things, it said crazy things, it appeared to have no rules, it had a lot of soul and the people who worked there worked there because they were *Caroline* DJs and not because they had an opportunity to be on the radio in England other than the BBC. And I think a lot of the *Radio London* chaps, not to knock them, but they were professional radio broadcasters, taking advantage of the fact that *Radio London* was there and they could work on it; whereas the *Caroline* jocks were there for the challenge of the whole thing because they believed that they could do something with that freedom. So *Caroline* I loved very much which was why I decided to run the risk of falling foul of the Marine Offences Act and stayed on after the act came in.

We felt we were very much part of an elite and we loved it, talk about an ego stroke. When we went on land and did personal appearances in discotheques we seemed to get more of a reaction from the audience than the groups would get and there we were, DJs basically just playing the records, but there was something about it and it wasn't just the fact that it was pirate radio, it was because of the time. It was because there was Carnaby Street, it was because The Beatles had come along with their long hair, waved two fingers to everybody else and said 'hey listen, we've got ideas and music and things to say and we're sick to death of being told shut up until you grow up and told you have nothing to say, we do have something to say, we do have ideas for the way we want to dress, we do have ideas of what is good music and we are going to have fun'. And it was such a wonderful time because imagine **Maggie Thatcher** now in this day and age actual praising Frankie Goes to Hollywood, whereas politicians like **Harold Wilson** fell over themselves to make a reference to The Beatles in their political speeches."

It was the Labour Government, however, that engineered the end of the pirate radio era with the Marine Offences Act, a fact which Walker tries to rationalise, although he has never forgiven Wilson

for that betrayal of trust . . .

"That was the time that everyone realised that there was such an energy and enthusiasm and exuberance coming from the young people that nobody could ignore them and everybody had to acknowledge the fact that it was there. But it was a Labour Government that decided that this freedom, this anarchy of the airwaves, should not continue and they brought in the Marine Offences Act, which was one of the great mistakes of all time as regards the media in this country.

What they did and I still to this day wonder if there was a Government conspiracy behind it, they decided to introduce the new law after the murder of **Reg Calvert** by **Smedley** — who pulled the trigger.

One has to be wary of conspiracy theories but the facts are these: that Reg Calvert was shot, Oliver Smedley pulled the trigger, Oliver Smedley got off. The moment that court case hit the newspapers it was 'This is what the pirates are really like, they are a bunch of crooks, they are the highwaymen of the high seas, don't let them try and fool you that they are raising money for charity or appealing to all age groups and doing nothing innocuous; they are wicked people, crooks and they should be stopped'.

It was only after that murder and court case that the Labour Government felt able to be able to push through a law that would turn off the pirates, so one has to be extremely suspicious of that whole murder and court case and everything that followed on. Had that not happened, had we had a more enlightened Government, a Government less worried about controlling everything and more interested in free enterprise then I think they might have said, 'we give *Radio Caroline* and *Radio London* and the others a Licence to operate on land and give them the opportunity to do it legally — and see what happens.' "

The leading disc jockeys of the period were enjoying a status somewhat akin to the musicians they played on air. By the time Walker came on board the *Mi Amigo* the presenters were well established as celebrities:

"It started Easter '64 and I joined in '66, so just over 2 years had gone. By that time it was quite established that the people who worked on it were stars in their own right, you joined knowing that that was the way it was. We very much enjoyed in a way living a double life, the one side of it was there we were glamour pirates, and we played up that side of it when we were on land. I remember **Robby Dale** and myself bought very expensive clothing from stores like Granny Takes a Trip in Kings Road and we had silver topped ebony canes. We just really went the whole hog and yet on the ship it was the other side of that double existence, a lot of time we'd roll up to the radio if we were on early in the morning in our pyjamas, we hadn't shaved, we were as scrawny as hell, so the day to day running of the ship, the reality of being on a boat, was far removed from how the public imagined it to be.

We would get incredibly bored. During the summer it wasn't so bad, you could go on deck and sun bathe, you would

get visitors come out a lot more in the summer. In the winter months, sometimes when storms were forecast we used to, in the old expression, batten down the hatches. All the windows in the living quarters on the top of the deck would be covered over with metal shutters and then it was like living in a submarine and it could be like that for three or four days at a time.

I wouldn't say I was a good sailor, but none of us really got sick actually on the ship, because it used to roll gently. The winds used to be strong and it used to lean at an angle for a long time, but there was no bobbing up and down in a small boat. Travelling to and from the ship, even though it only took an hour and a half from Felixstowe or Harwich a lot of us were violently ill. Then we really did get sick, but none of us got that sick on the boat."

When the Smedley affair hit the newspapers the sparkling world of the pirate radio companies became tarnished. Quite a few people agreed with Walker that there may be something going on behind the scenes. Was it possible that the big advertising income of some radio ships was attracting criminal elements? Walker discounts this extreme and concludes that as the companies became more experienced in the new medium, business ethics surfaced to curtail the extravagances of the pirate broadcasters:

"*Radio London* was a very professionally run organisation, it had a professional sound on the air and the administrative structure of the station was also very professional. You have to remember that it was all very new to people, it was a fun time, when record companies didn't know whether a record was going to be a hit or not, not like today where it is an investment of x thousand pounds for the video and whatever, all very cold business type. Then everybody was having a good time, it was great to be going, great to be alive, the 60s was an optimistic time, **Kennedy** was in the White House. The whole thing was so different, and I don't believe there was evil payola and criminal things going on, there wasn't.

Ronan was seemingly never really interested in money although a lot of the people who put money into the business, to make *Radio Caroline* possible, were your normal sources of big money, the City, Financiers, Merchant Bankers.

I'm not sure how wealthy he was himself, I think his idea was to leave Ireland to come and try and make it on his own. If you want to talk about the morality of big business, *Caroline* was no more bent than any giant corporation.

The Dutch company who supplied the crew, tenders, actual physical supplies of oil, food and water; the only time I know they were ripped off was post August '67 when **Ronan** wasn't really running *Caroline* it was run by somebody else and his policy seemed to be not to pay those bills to keep the ship running for as long as possible and to play records on his label and make as much money as possi-

ble. Prior to August '67 the Dutch company must have been getting paid otherwise they wouldn't keep doing it.

A Dutch company supplied *Radio England, Radio Caroline* and *Radio London.* The same tender used to come to the three boats from Holland, based in Felixstowe and Harwich. We didn't worry about all that anyway, we were young and having a good time.''

By the time the Marine Offences Act became law, many of the young radio men had become professional, or at least semi-professional, broadcasters. They looked to the landbased regular companies for employment, the self same companies that had been derided as being 'establishment', that great sixties expression of distaste. Not so Johnnie Walker, who believed earnestly in all the pirate ships had been trying to achieve:
"I think within my character there is an inbuilt love of freedom for the individual and an honest freedom, not the freedom to screw people or to hike people up. But it seemed to me that despite whatever slight underhand dealings might have gone on within the business structure of *Radio Caroline,* what went out over the air and why people listened in to it was a no bullshit. Honest. And I really believed that *Caroline* wasn't doing any wrong and I used to read all the letters I had time to read from people who listened in and they just loved the idea that people were there, saying what they felt like saying.

I never used to go on the air if I felt really down and say 'it's great out here, it's a lovely day', people see through that plasticity immediately. I would go on there and be myself, be honest and talk about things that I cared about, about the way music would affect me, whether it would make me sad, or whether it really excited me or whatever. And I had the freedom to be able to do that; to me it was only right that it should continue.

The idea then of the BBC, which was an organisation run by a massive faceless number of people who typed scripts and nothing was spontaneous, everything was organised and timed down to the last minute, to me it was just so bland, so uninteresting, so unexciting. Whereas *Caroline* on the other hand, we made our mistakes, we were stupid, but we were human above all and ourselves, and people could feel that by listening, you were listening to something that wasn't controlled, wasn't trying to be something other than what it was — that is a bunch of young people who were enjoying being alive in the 1960s. Enjoying playing some of the best music the world has ever produced pop music wise, and not being constrained in that enthusiasm and that communication. And that is why I felt that had got to continue for as long as possible.

I didn't think about career or future or what on earth I was going to do. I never believed *Caroline* would go off the air, I didn't even consider that, I was having such a good time, enjoying it so much and knowing the listeners were feeling the same, that if we can turn the transmitter on at 6 o'clock tomorrow, then that is what we will do.''

It was business and finance that put Walker off the air shortly afterwards when the Caroline Organisation ran into difficulties with the Dutch supply company. A commando like operation silenced the North and South units in one dawn swoop . . .

"In March of 1968 tugs were sent by the Dutch company that was supplying the boat, synchronised to arrive at *Radio Caroline North* and *Radio Caroline South* at five in the morning when the ship would be at its sleepiest. Boarded both the ships, cut the anchor chains and they were very heavy duty anchors to hold the ship in high seas and basically they stole both the ships and towed them to Amsterdam.

We had no warning of it, we weren't on the air so we couldn't say anything to our listeners, one day we were there just the same as always next day we were gone and apparently it was because the person who was running *Radio Caroline* at that time had not paid the bills that he should have paid.

Phillip Soloman, seemed to be in control of *Radio Caroline* he owned the record label called Major Minor Records and he hadn't paid the money to the Dutch company, owned by the Wijsmuller Brothers, and they waited and waited and asked and asked for the money and it didn't show up and they thought 'if that is the way the ball is being played we will go and steal the ships, tow them back to Amsterdam, sell the transmitters and make what we can out of it.'

So I was in Amsterdam, towed there by the tugs, waited there for three days to find out what was going to happen, nobody seemed to know anything, so I came back to London and that was the end of *Caroline* at that particular time.

There then followed a year out of work and I drove trucks for a living. The crazy thing was that that year I had scored quite heavily in the DJ polls; the News of the World had a poll after *Radio 1* came on, and apparently from what I heard I had come No. 1 in it, but of course, they couldn't have that so my name wasn't mentioned at all. I was No.3 in Record Mirror and Music Echo.

So there I was high up in the DJ poll, but out of work, couldn't get a job. The BBC, I later found out, had a policy that no one was to employ me on a programme until at least a year had passed of my final broadcast, until that taint of criminality had worn off. I remember driving a truck down Wood Lane, full of 8 track stereos delivering them to the West End, following this Aston Martin and as it passed BBC Television in Wood Land the driver blasted the horn and waved to everybody and I realised it was **Simon Dee**. I thought it really interesting, my following THE *Caroline* DJ and funnily enough the place I delivered those 8 track stereos to was 40 Hartford Street, right next door to *Radio Luxembourg* and I was putting on dark glasses and holding my head down as I staggered in with these boxes hoping that nobody on *Luxembourg* would recognise Johnnie Walker, star of *Radio Caroline* was a lorry driver. But I had to earn a crust and that is the way I did it.

After a year, in April 1969, I decided that despite all I

AT WONDERFUL RADIO ONE

had said about the BBC that there was no sign of any other radio coming on, it was five years before *Capital* started and if I wanted to stay in radio, I would have to go to the BBC. So I let it be known I was interested and they let it be known they were interested in me coming in so that is the way it started."

A structure like that of the BBC was everything that Walker had disapproved of and yet it wasn't long before he became embroiled in what is, after all, the greatest broadcasting system in the World. It needed some re-evaluations:

"You were very aware when you were sitting on the first floor of Broadcasting House that there are another seven floors above you with monitors tuned into *Radio 1* in every office, and it was so different, but you did have the power of broadcasting to the whole of the United Kingdom.

The system on *Radio Caroline* was — we had the National top 40 in the studio which was the best selling 40 singles of the week, we also had in there the American Hot 100 which was the top selling 100 singles. There wasn't much in the way of albums at that time, really albums only started to happen with Sergeant Pepper and The Beatles. So it was basically a singles radio station and the format was one in, one out, one record from the *Caroline* top 40, the next record would be anything you wanted, could be an oldie, could be a new single, an American hit single, it didn't matter.

The jock had complete freedom to play whatever he wanted. When I went to the BBC they had grown up with a producer who would choose a presenter to present the programme before the microphone, but the producer would choose what music was going to be played. So when the BBC started *Radio 1* it was a dramatic departure for them to have the presenter, a DJ, in so much more control. I mean on pirate stations we had self op boards as they are called, which is a DJ operating the turntables, microphone, tape cartridges that play the jingles and commercials, he would do the lot. On *Radio Caroline* would be a DJ, the equipment, wires going down to the transmitter, the limiter which stopped anything too loud going into the transmitter and the transmitter up to the aerial and into your radio. That is the way it was and basically that is all you need.

With the BBC having their system of producers, engineers, and all the rest of it, they agreed that they would have self operated boards for the DJ so we were starting our own turntables, but an engineer sitting the other side of the glass masterminding all the levels, the producer was hovering around with a stop watch in his hand, another fellow would be sitting there to play any tapes of groups because you couldn't play records all the time, all these things inhibit the spontaneity and freedom of the DJ. That is why radio people love radio rather than TV because on radio it is immediate, you don't have to rehearse it, you can just do it and that was the snag with the BBC, all this structure."

Walker left the BBC in June 1976 to work the airwaves in the USA. The reality of the American radio systems did not live up to his expectations however . . .
"I find America incredibly old fashioned in its attitude to music, because I went over there **Johnny Rotten** time, the Sex Pistols had been on Granada TV, that whole thing had happened, the whole new music movement was taking off in England and was filtering through very strongly into America. But America was just so steeped in denim, long hair, joints and rock and roll, typified by The Beatles, The Stones, The Who and Led Zeppelin, they couldn't think about playing any new stuff and they are still really, despite all that has happened, they are reluctant to enter into new things.

That is what did America for me, I thought for 6000 radio stations there must be opportunities to be a bit dangerous, to be creative to do innovative things.

I was disappointed, but I love the place. All I talked about the freedom of expression on *Radio Caroline* does exist in America, you can say a hell of a lot more on the radio than you can in this country, the press is very much more free, the rights of the individual are written into the Constitution which they are not in this country. There was a lot about the country that really appealed to me but after five years there I just had this yearning to come home."

Walker still feels a sympathy for the pirates of today and toyed with the idea of supporting Ronan O'Rahilly with the new *Caroline* venture. Like many of the original pirates, however, he feels his career must push forwards not backwards . . .
"Having been in America and having worked in places where there is so much choice on the radio, quite frankly I love the idea of lots of pirates coming on the air and stirring things up a bit. *Caroline* I wanted to be involved in when it re-started but **Ronan O'Rahilly** — I think his head is stuck in the 60s and he is very old fashioned musically and we had arguments about what music *Caroline* should play. When I saw basically he wanted just an album station of the type that I had just left in America, because I felt they were so stuck in this album type format, which is exactly what I was doing on the BBC in the 70s. There were some great albums being made and some grotty singles being made and I didn't want to play Bay City Rollers but I wanted to play Steely Dan or the Eagles or that kind of stuff. But things have changed now and there are less good albums being made and more good singles and I felt *Caroline* really had to be a new, innovative, basically a singles radio station, and that wasn't his idea at all.

I don't listen to *Caroline* much at all, basically I find it pretty uninteresting and irrelevant to the times. *Laser* I think is great although it can get boring when you listen for a long time because they don't say very much. I think it is great that it is there, music with no bullshit and they will play you all sorts of stuff, oldies, good new hits, **Jessie Brandon** I love — the girl DJ on there and I think it is good that stations like *Laser, Caroline* and various pirate stations are challenging the status quo of radio in this country. I think the IBA have failed the radio listener in that they haven't provided them with good interesting creative choices in the radio listening but with a very safe, stereo-typed radio station and — no choice.

Most ILR stations are like the old Light Programme, before *Radio 1*, and *2*, they try and be all things to all people and that is impossible and really there should be more radio. There is a lot of pressure now for community radio and there is a potential in TV of people being able to have a cable connected to their homes which would bring them 20 or 30 different TV channels and if you can have that wider choice in TV then I think you need to have a wider choice in radio.

I'm more interested in television now, in doing something different, because I've done just about all there is to do in radio all over the world. I'm doing something slightly different at this station (*Wiltshire Radio*), more news and interviews and stuff, not just introducing records, but I would like to do some television now because I think I could have a lot of fun doing that . . ."

1967

JAN 3 RADIO BBMS finally closes.

JA N 17 **Roy Bates** appears before Chelmsford Quarter Sessions to appeal against his £100 fine, without success.

JAN 23 A writ against **Cheeta II** is issued on behalf of the London & East Anglia Ship Supply Co., who want £3,000 for services and wages they supplied to the boat.

FEB 9 At Rochford Magistrates Court **Mrs Dorothy Calvert** is charged with contraveneing the 1949 Wireless Telegraphy Act. She claims that **Shivering Sands Fort** is outside the territorial limit, but this is rejected by the Magistrates. She is found guilty and fined £100.
That night the crew hear of the result and at midnight RADIO CITY finally goes off the air with 'The Party's Over' and the playing of the National Anthem.

FEB 10 RADIO 390 agrees to pay The Performing Rights Society a fee for music played on the station. **Ted Allebeury** resigns from the station. **David Lye** took over as Manager.

FEB 22 BRITAIN RADIO closes before opening again under the name RADIO 355.

FEB 24 At Rochford Magistrates Court the director of Estuary Radio and the station are found guilty on various counts of illegal broadcasting. The crucial evidence is provided by the Navy who show how far high tide extends on the Estuary and thus prove that **Red Sands** is within territorial waters. The station is fined £200, and each of the directors is fined £40.

MAR 13 City and County Commercial Radio (Scotland) Ltd and **Tommy Shields** are charged with broadcasting without licence. The company pleads guilty and is fined £80, **Tommy Shields** pleads not guilty, and this is accepted.

MAR 16 The Government moves the second reading of the **Marine etc., Broadcasting (offences) Bill. Mr. Short** the Postmaster General announces that the Government plans to provide more choice for listeners, by another popular music programme by the end of the year. There were also plans to provide further choice in nine selected areas, as a prelude to setting-up of a national system of local radio.

MAR 18 Peir-Vick the company who operates RADIO DOLPHIN and BRITAIN RADIO

goes into liquidation and is taken over by Carstead Advertising, headed by **Ted Allebeury**, formerly of RADIO 390. Both stations operating from the 480 ton ship **Laissez Faire**, have their names changed. RADIO DOLPHIN becomes RADIO 227, BRITAIN RADIO becomes RADIO 355.

APR 1 A new station, RADIO EAST ANGLIA, arrives on air testing on the same frequency as RADIO LONDON, interruptions continue all morning until it takes over completely. At about midday, RADIO LONDON takes over again, and RADIO EAST ANGLIA vanishes. The whole thing had been organised and produced on board **Galaxy** by RADIO LONDON DJs as a gigantic April Fools joke.

APR 7 The Comet anchors off Ballywalter, near Whitehad, Co. Antrim, N. Ireland. It changes name to RADIO SCOTLAND AND IRELAND, or RADIO 242.

MAY A survey carried out by a Swiss Company, Brown Boveri shows that the medium wave band could carry a further 115 low-power medium frequency stations, if all of them broadcast according to the ruling of the International Telecommunications Union in Geneva.

JUL 3 The Laissez Faire broadcasts a message that there is a man aboard threatening to kill the crew. The police at Clacton refuse to do anything as it is outside their jurisdiction. Engine trouble prevented the ship from sailing closer to shore.

JUL 4 In the early morning the tender **Offshore Two** brings men onto the **Laissez Faire**. Order is restored, and two men are taken off the

ship.

JUL 13 The BBC announces that their first local radio station will begin operations from Leicester on Nov. 8. RADIO SHEFFIELD on Nov 15, RADIO MERSEYSIDE on Nov 22nd, with others to follow in the New Year.

JUL 21 RADIO 227 closes.

JUL 28 After its final appeal has been lost RADIO 390 finally closes down at 5.00 pm with the news and the playing of Alan Price's 'The House That Jack Built' and the National Anthem — then silence. **Phillip Birch**, of RADIO LONDON issues a statement to say that: 'It is unfortunate that this Government's attitude towards independant radio has consistently been one of suppression as part of a determined plan to continue the Governments monopoly in radio broadcasting'. Accordingly it had been decided to close down RADIO LONDON.

AUG 6 A raid on **Red Sands** causes damage and theft valued at about £500. Five men are later held and charged in connection with the offence.
RADIO 355 closes. This is due to the expiry of the contract between Carstead Advertising Ltd, and the owners of RADIO 355 and the owners of the ship.

AUG 14 At midnight, RADIO SCOTLAND closes down. A close-down ball is held in the Locarno Ballroom, Glasgow.

LONG FACES AND SHORT SKIRTS MARK THE END OF PIRATE RADIO AS THEY KNEW IT — IN THE *RADIO LONDON* OFFICES

⚡ I WANT MY CAROLINE ⚡

RADIO 270 also closes, the intention had been for all the DJ's to be aboard the **Oceaan VII** but bad weather prevents this. A friend of one of the DJ's in the RAF is persuaded to drop a parcel containing a tape of the other DJ's saying their farewells onto the ship. The drop misses the ship, so **RADIO 270** closes without them. Later an official enquiry is launched into the use of an RAF helicopter for this purpose.

AUG 15 The Marine Broadcasting Offences Act becomes law. 3.00 pm **RADIO LONDON** closes with the Beatles 'A Day in the Life'. Thousands of fans gather at Liverpool Street Station, to welcome **RADIO LONDON'S** DJ's after the station closed down. Many of the fans wear black arm-bands, and badges with 'Wilson for ex-premier' on them.

AUG 15 The **CAROLINE** organisation opens an office in Holland at Singel 160, Amsterdam. On board the **Mi Amigo** are **Johnnie Walker**, **Spangles Muldoon**, **Ross Brown** and **Robbie Dale**. **CAROLINE** broadcasts continue despite M.O.A.

AUG 21 The M.O.D. begins the destruction of ex-army forts, in order to prevent them being used by interest other than the Ministry.
The **Galaxy** arrives in Hamburg, and painted white. It is bought by an ad agency Gloria International of St. Gallen.

AUG 31 The Manx Parliament, The House of Keys, reluctantly ratifies the **Marine Broadcasting Offences Act** at 8.30 pm bringing it into line with the mainland. It becomes effective from midnight.

At Midnight DJ **Don Allan** announces 'This is the Northern Voice of **RADIO CAROLINE INTERNATIONAL** on 259 meters, the continuing voice of free radio for the British isles.'

SEPT 30 BBC radio takes on a new look: Radio One comes on air on 247 meters — the new pop music service. It is staffed with ex-pirate DJ's, such as **Tony Blackburn**, **Dave Cash**, **John Peel**, **Emperor Rosko**, **Duncan Johnson** and **Stuart Henry**.

NOV 8 Lloyds report **Cheeta II** leaves Flushing heading for Spain.

NOV 13 **Cheeta II** leaves Corunna in Spain bound for Morocco (arrives in Safi on Nov 18).

NOV 21 **Cheeta II** leaves Safi in Morocco for the Canary Islands.

NOV 24 **Cheeta II** arrives in Tenerife.

DEC 3 **Cheeta II** leaves for Las Palmas. **RADIO SYD** is granted a licence in The Gambia and broadcats are made from land on 910 kHz (329 meters). **Cheeta II** is moored in Bathurst Harbour and used as a restaurant.

JAN 27 While helping in the search of a lost man, the **Tiri** loses her own moorings in the dark. Engine failure forces the ship to drift towards the coast at Whangaparapara. In the attempts to free her she is damaged further. Eventually she is towed clear by the tug Sea Toiler.

RADIO VERONICA hires time on **RADIO POPULARIE DE MALLORCA** to test for a series of programmes along the Spanish coast. Back home a Swiss station on the same wave length badly affects night time reception.

FEB 2 An examination reveals that extensive damage to the **Tiri** has made her unfit for future use.

FEB 24 Work begins on the **Kapuni**, now renamed **Tiri 2**. She is 101 foot long and weighs 194 tons.

FEB 28 **RADIO HAURAKI** restarts broadcast.

MAR 2 A heavy Dutch tug anchors a mile away from **CAROLINE NORTH** and refuses any form of communication. 10pm: **Don Allen's** show ends with Jim Reeves and after watching TV most of the crew turn in.

MAR 3 2am: Dutch seamen from the tug invade the **CAROLINE NORTH** and hold everyone on board prisoner. The leader reads a message to the senior staff from the tender firm of **Wijsmuller** instructing a complete close down of the station. To avoid violence the staff comply. 6pm: The tug, the **Utrecht**, takes **The Fredericia** under tow for Amsterdam. On arrival the staff are paid and given 'plane tickets for England. It was the last they were to hear from the station bosses.

MAR 3 The tug **Titan** pulls up alongside **RADIO CAROLINE SOUTH**. Half way through their hours warm up the station goes off air at 5.20 am. Crew from the tug representing the **Wijsmuller Brothers**, seize and tow the **Mi Amigo** into Amsterdam.

APR 9 Winds, reaching hurricane force pound the coast of the North Island forcing the **Tiri 2** to shelter.

APR 10 The **Tiri 2** breaks moorings and is beached. However she is towed clear again, and the damage caused in the storm repaired.

APR 15 **RADIO HAURAKI** returns to the air.

AUG 15 One year after the Act outlawing pirate radio stations, **RADIO LONDON THREE** transmits for one hour on 204 meters. The occasion is also marked by an all-night vigil outside the G.P.O. in St. Martins-le-Grand EC1. A coffin is borne through the strees of London with 'the mortal remains of pirate radio' and ends in Downing Street, where a letter of protest is delivered. Later it is discovered that the aerial was hitched to the fire-escape of the BBC offices in Richmond Way, Shepherds Bush.

Over the following days, **RADIO LONDON THREE** continues intermittent broadcasts, renamed **RADIO FREE LONDON**. In one raid G.P.O. engineers raid a flat where DJ **Spangles Muldoon** is broadcasting, they confiscate a bogus machine, leaving the real equipment intact!

OCT **RADIO VERONICA** carries out tests on 538 meters to avoid Swiss interference and an FM transmitter is considered.
Work on the **Galaxy** is continuing and a new station is announces for the 1st November, to broadcast from 5-10 on 266 meters.

NOV 1 The announced date for the new German station on board **Galaxy** fails to materialise. It is put back by another month.

DEC 1 Still nothing is heard from **Galaxy**.

1969

JAN 25 Aware of the imminent passing of the German Marine Offences Act. Gloria International bosses **Norbert Gschwendt** and **Emile Luthle** withdraw their financial backing from the **Galaxy**.

MAR 19 **RADIO JACKIE** begins broadcasts on 227 meters,

directing their show to an audience in South West London. It is run by 17 year old **Mike Knight**.

MAR 20 **VERONICA'S** land base moves to bigger studios in the Utrechtsweg. During the move production continues using both studios.

AUG 23 A Company, **CAPITAL RADIO** is formed by the International Broadcasters Society. Over the next few months a web of companies are to be formed, centred in Lichtenstein.
The Company purchases a 148 foot long 359 ton coaster, **The Zeevaart**, and has it refitted, with a 10Kw transmitter from **RADIO 270**, in Zaandam.
The ship is renamed **King David**, and is registered in Lichtenstein. It is the first ship to fly the Lichtenstein flag.

A KNIGHT IN DISGUISE

THE KING DAVID AND CURIOUS ANTENNA

TONY PRINCE

Tony Prince is one of the most successful jocks to have come from pirate radio, and it is due to his sheer determination to succeed that has put him where he is today. As Managing Director of the *Disco Mix Club*, amongst other music business interests, Tony continues to involve himself in helping develop the DJ industry, music, and the encouragement of young people anxious for a career in that most extravagant of options — music radio.

Tony Prince was born Tommy Whitehead, the only son of Frank and Kathleen, on May 9th 1946, in Oldham Lancs. At his Secondary Modern school he was already beginning to develop his talents for the off-beat, zany character he was later to become — he was much more interested in flicking pellets and creating mayhem than in receiving an education.

At 13 years of age he entered Oldham Municipal Art School, less interested in Art than in the latest pop records, he bought himself an acoustic guitar for £6.10s and practised singing hits in front of the mirror. At fifteen he became an apprentice jockey at the Middleham racing stable of Gerald Armstrong, but a six-month stint with little pay, long hours and back-breaking work soon convinced Tony that racing was not for him.

He got a job at Oldham Co-Op, in the Radio Department, and began to play records at one of the local dance halls — The Princess — every Saturday night, for 7s. 6d. That Summer he took his usual holiday at Butlins in Wales. One night he got chatting to the drummer of the resident group — Rory Storm and The Hurricanes, who advised him to enter the next nights talent contest. Assisted by a triple Scotch, Tony proceeded to wow the audience with an over-the-top rendition of a popular song, 'Mean Woman Blues', while at the same time unintentionally giving a first rate impression of a bull in a china shop: falling over the mike-wire, and in one attempt at gymnastics, losing one of his boots.

The audience loved it, and he got second prize. Two lads from Oldham were in the audience: they had a band — The Silver Dollars — but no singer, so they invited Tony to join. The man responsible for unleashing this mayhem on the world, that cowboy-booted drummer, was later to achieve certain fame for himself as Ringo Starr.

After gigging for a while the band was re-named The Jasons, and under that name played regularly at the local dance hall — The Savoy. Their big chance came when they were offered a residency at a Butlins camp, but members of the band, having secure regular jobs, refused. Upset, Tony left and got himself a plum job as vocalist for the band at Oldham's new Top Rank — The Johnny Francis Orchestra. When the resident DJ didn't turn up one night, the manager asked Tony to fill in and spin some records. The band, with Tony, moved to Bristol to the prestige Top Rank venue, the Bristol Suite. Here an argument with the Musicians Union officer about playing recorded music led to his expulsion from the Union — perforce he had become a full-time DJ.

As always he was his own best publicist — arranging to be kidnapped by students and ransomed... playing records in a shop window, and being almost arrested for obstruction. He left the Bristol Suite to start his own band — The Tony Prince Kombo — but left when they all went off to find fame and fortune in Germany.

He went back to the Bristol Suite, but then got a call from Chris Mercer of TWW Television, to do an audition for the TWW pop show, Discs-A-Go-Go. He got the job and worked there for 18 months. Tony Blackburn, his co-compere, was just starting on *Caroline*, when his job at TWW came to an end, Prince too found himself on the ocean aboard *Caroline North*.

He was quickly given the sack when a new programme director thought him unsuitable. It was only at the insistence of the many fans he had generated in his brief period on board which led to Ronan O'Rahilly giving him the job back. *Caroline* allowed his naturally piratical nature to come to the fore. While it is true to say that life on board was not always full of smiles, Tony took to it, and as before, the pranks were a constant diversion from the humdrum reality of ship life.

One particular joke almost went wrong when a new crew member was told that as a novice on board he had to 'walk the plank'. Despite his protests he was made to do it.

the occasional disco work later, *Luxembourg* called to offer him a job as DJ. So off to the Grand Duchy he went.

At this time *Luxembourg* began to experience an unprecedented boom. This was in part due to the dearth of alternatives, it was also due to the fans of the various pirate DJs following their idols to the new frequency. Tony was well paid by most standards, and along with the other English-speaking members, he had an enviable lifestyle. Clubs open into the small hours had their own special fascination to the jocks more used to the archaic British licensing laws, and meant a night-life which was varied and exciting.

In November 1970 he left with the idea of dipping into the deeper pond of American radio. But the pregnancy of his wife gave cut short this plan, and he was soon back on the airwaves. He got himself involved in the massive publicity that triggered the Osmonds fame, by going to the USA to tape five shows with the group. These were played on *Luxembourg* prior to the Osmonds' arrival in Britain. Tony Prince joined them throughout the tour and kept the fans informed about all the minutiae of life on tour.

In 1977 Tony returned to London, to Hertford Street, to take up a post as *Luxembourg* programme director, while keeping his job as DJ. This led to a lot of commuting. It was Tony who helped persuade the station to drop its album format, and change it to a more disco-oriented beat.

After fifteen years with *Radio Luxembourg*, in 1983, Tony Prince finally left to concentrate on his own projects in the music business, injecting them with twenty years expertise and the Regal Ruler's own brand of energy.

As a piece of bravado he dived in, and before anyone knew it was starting to drown. Tony dived in to rescue him, but despite being an excellent swimmer, was himself caught in the man's desperate clutch. It took another crew member to save the situation.

Another time a crew member fell and hurt his ankle. Again he was a newcomer to the ways of the ship, and the captain had little trouble in convincing him that the injury was much worse than it was. The 'broken' leg was bandaged and the unfortunate man was confined to bed with his leg hoisted up in the air. After a period he was told that it had deteriorated even further to the point where amputation might be necessary. In this sorry state he was put aboard the next tender to dry land, and sent to a doctor with a letter of explanation. The crewman never lived down the joke...

In Summer life was very pleasant — sunbathing and swimming were relaxing pastimes. On a swimming race around the ship with a member of the Dutch crew, the Regal Ruler found himself in a close embrace with a Portugese Man-of-War jellyfish. Two days of illness followed, leaving him forever with a reluctance to go swimming on that particular stretch of coast.

Tony also spent a brief period aboard *Caroline South*. At one point when the mast-wiring broke loose the two Tony's (Blackburn and Prince) drew the short straws, and had to climb up and fix it because the professional riggers wouldn't risk the bad weather.

Like many of the pirates, Tony decided that with the passing of the Marine Offences Act, it was time to call a halt to his days on ship. A few months of frustration and

PETER BOWMAN

RADIO SCOTLAND
RADIO 270

LOCAL (WEST INDIES)
VARIOUS (ILR)
VARIOUS (AUSTRALIA)

Pete 'Boots' Bowman was another jock who just happend to be in the right place at the right time for his introduction to offshore broadcasting. It was a career he followed with increasing success until he quit radio to attend to family committments. He never returned to broadcasting although he had joined the pirate action at a very early stage...

"I come originally from Carlisle, which is almost Scotland but not quite, when I left school I went into journalism and I worked for the local newspaper, there were two local newspapers and I worked for the second one, a weekly and it wasn't much cop. From there I was offered something by Border Television, an ITV station up there, just a freelance job and I suppose you could say I got a taste for

broadcasting from that, not only for broadcasting but I had always been interested in music. I used to write columns in the paper that I worked for. The break for pirate radio... I used to do some ballroom DJ work in Newcastle which didn't pay very much — also I had to go from Carlisle three times a week.

I can't remember how I got that, just through somebody I knew in Carlisle who knew someone in Newcastle. There was a guy called **Roger Gale**, who is now an MP. He was a pirate DJ who worked for *Radio Caroline North* and he came to do a special night at the *Top Rank* ballroom in Newcastle, they did a *Caroline* night.

No one had ever heard of *Radio Caroline* in Newcastle, because it was all West coast and that was East coast. He said if ever he was in a position to, he would offer me a job and I thought 'oh yes'. Then he became programme director of *Radio Scotland* and sure enough sent me a telegram. I was very surprised because I wasn't much cop, I was bloody awful.

I had only met him once, but he was as good as his word and sent the telegram off, I don't know whether he was desparate or what, but he had this peculiar collection of people lined up for *Radio Scotland* one of whom was **Stuart Henry** who had been an actor, there was **Paul Young** who had also been an actor and still is. Someone else was a bus driver; a couple of other people, a sales director, all sorts of people. I don't know why he offered me a job, he didn't know me, he didn't hear much of me and I wasn't very good in the ballroom because it was a totally different scene."

Tommy Shields' radio project was, literally, a hulk. As an ex-lightship it had no engines and had to be towed everywhere, a fact which caused the *Comet* endless expense and difficulties. There are various memories of *Radio Scotland*, Mark Wesley remembers the powerful signal and solid station reputation; Bowman was onboard slightly earlier in the life of the far North's premier signal . . .

"When we arrived at *Radio Scotland* originally, there was no ship at all, it had to be towed up from wherever it was, Ireland or somewhere, so it was two or three weeks before we even saw it. Then it was thought it wasn't going to arrive after all, that it was going bust and all sorts of things. Eventually it arrived and it went on air on New Years Eve 1965/66, so we were all out there, what a way to spend New Years Eve, we were all out there on this terrible boat, lurching.

It was absolutely filthy, nothing was prepared in advance, there was no engine, it was the middle of winter so no one was very happy about it, particularly me."

Despite such alien conditions Bowman was one of those presenters who survived with little or no real discomfort, the first step in surviving a career as DJ. The second was dealing with the owners and their idiosyncratic ideas for this 'new' medium:

"Funnily enough, everybody looked at me and thought 'oh my God he is pale and thin and he will be off the boat in 24 hours' and I was one of the few who did not suffer at all. I never had sea sickness, ever, unlike **Stuart Henry,** of course, it was painful to watch. If he was doing his shift he was actually doing it, he didn't cry off and lie in the bunk he really did it. There were quite a few people like this who suffered from seasickness, who were on the ship five minutes and never heard of again.

Shields was alright. I didn't have a lot to do with him, I had an interview with him when I first went up to *Radio Scotland* with **Roger Gale** present; funnily enough when they were sitting talking, interviewing me, there was

a telephone call for Tommy and it turned out, he kept calling this guy Mike on the phone and it turned out this was **Mike Ahearn** looking for a job and I thought 'what the hell does he want to come up here for from *Radio Caroline*'; and I actually liked him.

I sounded very similar to him in many ways and I thought 'thank God he is not coming', because they didn't offer him a job.

He was a top *Caroline* man, then he went out to Australia, I heard him in Australia when I was out there, he works for *4BC Brisbane* or he did, I don't know whether he does now. He was excellent, he really was. He was very very funny, very distinctive.

I just went out there (Australia) as a import, back in '69 I think it was, I was persuaded to go by **Noel Miller**, or **Neddy Noel** as he was called, he worked for *270*. He said if I ever went out there he would sponsor me, which does help and I stayed with him and his wife for quite a long time before I got anywhere.

Tommy Shields, he was a strange character, I don't even know why he was in the radio business because he wasn't going to make any money out of it, I don't think he ever did.

He ran some publicity company, his name was **Thomas V. Shields**, and it was called TVS Publicity and he knew what he was doing, but he had some very grandiose ideas that never came off. He had incredible schedules he had worked out for what *Radio Scotland* was going to be."

The *Comet* went down in the annals of radio ships as a floating disaster, although it seemed to be circumstances beyond the control of Tommy Shields that affected the station. It was, however, hugely popular in the Northern parts of England it could be heard:

"We had a programme director, **Roger** and his deputy who was **Bob Spencer**, he did all the schedules and everything — but it was all mapped out . . .

I say format, it wasn't much of a format really, you more or less had your own free choice as to what you played within the music that he wanted at any particular time of day, but it wasn't always adhered to. People used to play anything sometimes.

It had constant transmitter trouble and signal trouble, we weren't getting into Glasgow because the boat was based on the East coast at a place called Dunbar, which was a funny place to put it because it is never going to get into Glasgow. You would have thought it would have been round the West coast, which it eventually did, but there were so many problems.

With no engine in the ship we had literally to tow it all the way over the top of Scotland. Of course it was the worst part of the year, with storms, there was a fire on board and goodness knows what else.

It was shocking weather up there. There was one particular episode where there was a flood in the hold and

the pumps just weren't operating successfully and they had to send ashore for a bilge pump. In fact they had to go it over the public airways which was pretty drastic to say 'we need a bilge pump, we are going off the air', instead of doing it on the radio telephone. They did it over the air and this thing eventually came out on the tender bouncing up and down and it was very scarey.

But the business about towing the ship over the top of Scotland, I wasn't on it, because I refused. This is when my decline with Tommy Shields started because I said 'I'm not going on there, there shouldn't be anybody on board', because they were supposed to be transmitting all the way round. I couldn't see the bloody point, the signal was fading, as it left Dunbar it would fade and after all who the hell lives on the top of Scotland apart from a few sheep.

Then it got into the West coast and that was the beginning of the troubles because it was too close to the shore. This is when the prosecutions began I believe, I wasn't there at the time but I gather they were within territorial waters. That is when his troubles really began.''

The organisation of *Radio Scotland* **was reputedly busy lobbying government for some deal whereby they would act as an official station for the North. Shields' costs were rising like the tide however, after his fatal move to the West Coast. Boots Bowman lost his enthusiasm for the circus and was fired, to find himself another job on the** station taking Yorkshire by storm — *Radio 270*. . .

''Tommy Shields, myself and a couple of other people went out to the boat when it was off Troon and they took another anchor out with them and when they released it I think someone was injured, I can't remember, he just didn't get away fast enough, an awful business really.

As we were all in the same boat, there was rivalry because there always will be, I think most people got on quite well. Bob Spencer had a terrific ego and seemed to have to do everything. He always got the biggest mail on the ship, but there was a reason for that because he did the biggest slot, breakfast.

There were sackfuls of mail, more so than the other one I went to which is *270* which had hardly anything, but then it was discouraged. But *Scotland* made the mistake, I think it is a mistake which is still prelevant in British radio today and that is these endless requests and dedications, reeling off names and addresses; that is what turns me off listening to radio today, it drives me crazy. It is all very well for the people who were recipients of the requests, but for everybody else it is just a bore. I tried not to do them at all, but Bob when he did the breakfast show used to do them between every record, it slows it all down and I could never stand that.

I got the push from *Radio Scotland*; there was one morning I was supposed to. . . I used to do to midnight and I was supposed to do the morning news from 5.30 am onwards and I thought it was a bit unfair; all it involved was taping the Light Programme or something off a VHF FM transmission, taping and re-writing it, it was a load of old rubbish. I was woken up and I just didn't get up, so poor old Bob didn't have any news that morning and I was told by Tommy Shields. I think he had decided that I was going to go anyway with this other thing and not being on the ship when they went round the top of Scotland.

I can't remember how I went to *270*, anyway I went down there and saw a guy called **Don Robinson** who was the director, it was in Scarborough and this other guy who is also an MP called **Wilf Proudfoot**. He was a very strange man and I didn't hit it off with him straight away but he got to like me after a while.

When I met Wilf Proudfoot, the station was run from his house, he took me down to the quayside to the supply boat and this tender was even worse than the one we had had on *Radio Scotland.* We had to climb down the quay and they were flinging bags down and I thought out aloud 'my God, another uncivilised set up'; and I heard this roar 'we are bloody civilised here and don't you forget it', and that was my introduction to Wilf Proudfoot, but after a few weeks he actually liked me.''

At the Scarborough station, onboard the Dutch lugger *Oceaan 7,* **Pete Bowman became forever 'Boots' Bowman. Widely popular,** *270* **was perhaps the station that was most essentially the precursor of current landbased operations like** *Radio Jackie.* **It's owners are still leading figures in local entertainment today.**
"I used to wear a pair of pigskin boots on the boat more or less all the time, I lived in them. There was another guy called **Tony Meehan** and he used to wear this peculiar collection of hats and he got the nickname The Hat, I suppose it was similar to that.

If the weather was rough it used to up anchor and go down to Bridlington, because it was a sheltered bay and they would go back again in the morning.

The funny thing is the boat itself was worse than *Radio Scotland,* it did have an engine but it was very subject to pitch and roll, very much so, more than *Radio Scotland.*

Anyway it used to pitch alarmingly from port to starboard or vice versa and it was quite a scarey boat. We used to have people come out and go round it, and they thought 'is this it, do they live here'. . . ."

The experience of *270* **was more enjoyable for Bowman because the owners were sold on the concept of professionalism, and this extended to the men doing the actual broadcasting job. On board were DJs of some experience hired from Australia, a common recruiting source at the time:**
"It was more fun than *Radio Scotland* because it was more. . . they had two Australian guys, programme controller and his deputy and they had worked on commercial radio for yonks and it was far more professional.

The actual format was Top 40, and you had to play strictly to this, unlike *Radio Scotland* where you tended to play more or less what fell out of the cupboard next, but here it was strictly controlled and sometimes we didn't like this but it was far better and much more professional.

If you wanted to run that kind of station that is the way it had to be done. The records you would play would be decided by the programme controller, not everybody, and often you would wish 'why aren't we playing this, or that', but the bug bear with that was that the play list used to come out and if Noel wasn't on the ship then that same list went on for two weeks instead of one. He would be setting up a new playlist back on shore. You would read the music papers and find The Four Tops, *Reach Out I'll Be There* was Number One and we would still have it at nine or something. Then he would come out with a brand new play list which was wonderful, all these new records would arrive.

Going back to *Radio Scotland,* all the records used to come out on the ship regardless and they would all be plonked in Bob Spencer's cabin and people would sneak in and just play them, they weren't supposed to, but I think that must be what is missing today. To-day nobody would dream of it. The new Beatles had to be played immediately, can you imagine anybody doing that now, they wouldn't give a damn, if it comes it comes, if it doesn't it doesn't.

I remember *Paperback Writer* came out and the tender arrived specially to bring this one record and I was on the air at the time and everybody was grabbing it like gold to bring it round to me to play. The bloody thing was warped and was bouncing up and down and it still played, but I can't imagine that now, nobody is that bothered, who is there around? Frankie Goes to Hollywood maybe? who everybody would be grabbing and dying to play. I can't think it would happen.

Everybody is too knowing now, too blasé.

It was very exciting, because you didn't really expect it to be. With *Radio Scotland* when it first went on the air we thought hardly anyone would listen but when people came out, **Tony Meehan**, he was just in sales at that time and eventually became a DJ, he came in grinning all over his face. 'You wouldn't believe the phone calls you have had in the first two weeks on the air', and they came out with all this mail and we couldn't believe it, sackfuls of the stuff. You thought even though it had advanced publicity, nobody it going to listen to this, it will take months to catch on.''

270 **was on air when Bowman joined and the company structure was being tested out, he stayed until the writing on the wall read 'closedown'. He had already lined up another job through his agent, in the West Indies, and as the pirates sank left the country.**
"*270* were just testing, the first person I saw when I got on board was Roger Gale and I said 'why are we off the air' and Roger looked at me and said 'do you feel you have

been somewhere before', it was very familiar: 'off the air', when we arrived and no chance of going back on, but something had gone wrong with the transmitter. Roger was programme director there...

There was no real money problem there, both stations (*270* and *Scotland*) it was ok. People had all sorts of funny ideas that if you weren't on the air they didn't pay you, it was all controlled just like any other company, they were both limited companies and they just paid you in the same way as anybody else would pay, with a pay slip.

It is still an important part of my life, I would not have missed it for the world. It was very exciting at the time, because then it was the sort of thing you dreamed of, you had heard about America and all these countless radio stations they had and we thought we would never get that here because you either listen to the Beeb or you don't listen.

When I first caught *Caroline* I was in Carlisle and we heard it was coming round from Frinton, and I thought 'I wonder if we will hear it here', but it was so clear it was incredible, all day 6.00 am to 6.00 pm and hearing music all day, it was something we had never heard before. If we wanted pop there was *Luxembourg* at night and that was all, with these hurried little quarter hours, the records sponsored by record companies and the record played only half way through. To hear this constant pop music it was incredible. Then you switched to the Light Programme and they were doing Workers Playtime, so you couldn't really miss.

Caroline was the first, and then all these piddly ones that came and went, and then *Scotland*...

It was supposed to be about 20kW, it had two 10kW RCA transmitters, whether they ever reached that I very much doubt but it had a good range, because my parents heard it in Carlisle and we had letters from somewhere in the Midlands, Kidderminster, who heard it at night.

There was a lot of huffing and puffing from the Government, **Tony Benn** came out with these odd things, he was the Minister of Post and Tele-Communications. I had an inkling towards the end of '66, because I was offered a job in the West Indies, which I took. It wasn't very successful, but that is by the by, but I took that at the end of '66 and the pirates were scuppered next August. That was the time I thought 'if I don't take this, I might find myself out of a job quickly'.

I had an agent in London which not so many people had, a girl called **Sharon Griffiths,** a Canadian, and she knew me through Roger Gale, because she was his agent as well and he put me onto her. I was always telling her to look out for other jobs, obviously it would have been nice to work for *Radio London* or *Radio Caroline* or anywhere. And she got this job with what was called Ross Radio Productions, they used to produce shows for *Luxembourg* and they did the English end of this station in the West Indies, which was also half French. That is how I got the job.

It was a dreadful station, I don't know what it is like now, I have no idea, but Monserrat has become the *in*

ANOTHER 'FUN' PROMOTION IDEA

place because there is a big studio there today.

I was there on a years contract, and I didn't renew it, it was pretty deadly. The company itself was French and Spanish and the English end was purely there because the Government in Monserrat insisted if it was going to be based on their island, which was a British island, that part of the transmissions had to be in English. That was the reason, and they just tolerated us, because they wanted it in French the whole time.

A 250kW station for two islands, Guadeloupe and Martinique, the rest were English, so that was it and it was a dreadful station..."

THE OCEAAN 7 OFF SCARBOROUGH

dle time, you can play anything, you don't pay royalties for this that and the other, record companies are willing for stations to play and flog them, all you pay for is the usual fees but no needle time.''

Bowman left the radio business on his return from the West Indies, an enforced holiday from the radio waves. His career in Australia, following emigration, blossomed only to be cut short by a serious illness in his family in England. Pete Bowman left Australia to be with his ailing mother and in doing so turned his back on the radio career he had worked so hard to build up there. He works now for Trust House Forte in London.

I was out for quite a while until I went to Australia, which is '69, so I was in Monserrat '67 until the beginning of '68. I was out for one and a half years and I worked for all sorts of people: Decca, a roller skating rink in Leeds, discos, and doing part time things for the BBC local stations *Radio Durham* and *Radio Leeds.* These were just half hours, just to say I was still in radio because it is quite a come down if you are working on air then you come back and find the place had changed that much, there were no pirates they had all gone, and there was only *Radio 1,* which was pretty dreadful at the time.

There was no chance of getting in there and that is when I decided I would emigrate.

I didn't have any relatives there, I just knew **Neddy Noel**, I stayed with him and his wife and he had already left the business. He was a butcher and his wife said to me when she met me at the airport 'you've got to have a word with Neddy' and I said 'why, what the hell is wrong with Neddy', and she said with this broad Aussie accent 'you know he's not in the radio business anymore', and I said 'no, he didn't mention it'. She said 'he's running a bloody butchers I have nightmares about meat' and I said 'what do you want me to do'; so she said 'persuade him to get out of it, I married a radio announcer'. I thought to myself 'I thought you married Noel'.

A couple of years later they divorced.

I always seemed to be relying on other people, it is the old maxim: It's not what you know, but who you know; he got me introductions to people in Melbourne.

I went to this radio station in Melbourne called *3XY* which at that time was lowest rated. A guy called **Dick Hemey** said 'no I can't do anything for you at the moment, but as it so happens I have a programme which goes out on Sundays called the London Scene, it is done for us by *Radio Luxembourg,* someone called **Don Wardell**, and he is sick this week. Would you like to do that live'.

I did that for two Sundays which was only half hour, but nothing actually followed on because he told me honestly it sounded authentic with my English accent. All you were doing was reading news items out of the music newspapers, but he said 'when you broaden your accent slightly come back and see me', but I never did.''

America still loomed large on the horizon for many English jocks and the method of getting there, assuming that a post with a BBC station had not materialised, was *Luxembourg* **or Australia. Quite a few gave up for good.**
''I thought it *(270)* **was bound to go soon and what would we all do, there would be all these people on the market all looking for jobs. I thought if I go with this one it might be a stepping stone to America.**

My tapes didn't impress anybody at *Radio Luxembourg.''*

Jan sent my audition tapes off everywhere, I think it was only **Paul Burnett** that made it to *Luxembourg.* At that time they were still having these half hours with record company sponsors where unless you were a station announcer you were London based, recorded programmes here and they were sent over.

Paul got a job, home based obviously as a station announcer there, but he went to *Manx Radio* first.

That was another awful station, I did go for an interview there and it sounded dreadful, at *Manx Radio* — it was the first legal commercial station, they had this awful needle time problem where only one record in ten was a commercially available record. This has been the bane of British radio for so long and it doesn't occur anywhere else in the world.

I went to Australia and there is no such thing as nee-

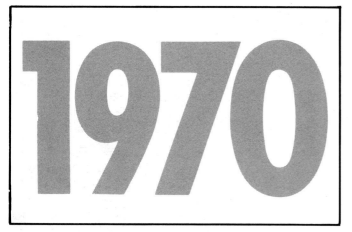

JAN 23 First test transmissions from **RADIO NORTHSEA INTERNATIONAL** begin at 10.30 pm. They start on 6210 kHz (49 MB SW) and 102 kHz FM.

FEB 9 It is announced that a new station will open using the transmitters of **RADIO MONTE CARLO**. It is to be called **RADIO GERONIMO**, and would play rock/progressive music, on 205 meters medium wave.

FEB 11 First tests for **RNI** medium wave band begin on 1610 kHz (186 meters).

FEB 28 6pm: **RADIO NORTHSEA INTERNATIONAL, (RNI)** aboard the 600 ton **Mebo II** in international waters begins broadcasting 20 hours of non-stop pop, on 186 (medium) and 102 kHz FM. German programmes are broadcast from 6.00 am to 8.00 am and 6.00 pm to 8.00 pm. English programmes are broadcast from 8.00 am to 6.00 pm and 8.00 pm to midnight.

MAR 7 Investigators from the Ministry of Posts and Telecommunications search among the hundreds of small boats on Ullswater in the Lake District in search of **RADIO LAKELAND**, which began broadcasting at the weekend on 197 meters.

MAR 24 Mebo II anchors off Clacton, but this causes interference to Walton-on-the-Naze coastguards.

MAR 27 RNI closes its medium wave but continues its FM broadcast.

APR 1 RNI goes off the air altogether.

APR 10 RNI returns on the same FM frequency as before, but changes to 190 meters medium wave.

APR 15 The Ministry of Posts and Telecommunications starts jamming from a naval radio station in Rochester, Kent.

MAY 1 RADIO VERONICA goes 24 hour on Fridays, Saturdays and Sundays. The station also raises 1,000,000 Guilders for the Kidney Foundation of Holland. Listeners requests were played for a 2.50 Guilder fee.

The first test are heard from **CAPITAL RADIO** on 270 meters. It consists of a portion of the BBC World Service.

RADIO GERONIMO claims that it is attracting an audience of over 2 million. It is not going to accept outside adverts but is going to start a mail-order service for its listeners, starting with records. It plans to increase its broadcasting time (3 hours a week, every Saturday) to 4 hours each night.

JUN 1 RADIO HAURAKI ceases to broadcast from the **Tiri 2**. It has been granted a licence by the New Zealand Government. The station transfers to Auckland, and begins its life as a legitimate station on 26 Sept 1970. It must be one of the few pirate ships to make this transition.

JUN 13 RNI changes its name to **RADIO CAROLINE INTERNATIONAL**, and broadcasts complete with **CAROLINE** jingles.

JUN 14 A rally followed by a march to Downing Street is held in Trafalgar Square in support of the station, led by **Ronan O'Rahilly.**

King David has by now anchored off Noordwijk in Holland and **CAPITAL RADIO** re-starts test broadcasts.

JUN 20 RADIO CAROLINE INTERNATIONAL reverts to being RNI and tries to dodge the increased jamming activity by changing frequencies.

JUL 1 Today is announced as the opening date of **CAROLINE TELEVISION.**It is to be broadcast from an airborne Super Constellation aircraft, based in Yugoslavia. It is to be on UHF, and in colour. The station fails to appear on the screen.

JUL 2 The Queen's Speech contains a promise that the Government would introduce local radio stations 'under the general supervision of an independent broadcasting authority'.

RADIO GERONIMO claims that the BBC transmitter at Folkestone is jamming its signal. Two of the **GERONIMO** DJ's pelt Broadcasting House with jam as a protest.

JUL 6 **Mr Christopher Chathaway** defends the jamming of illegal broadcasts, despite his admission that it costs about £1,200 a week to continue (£500 of which, he says, is in payment to Securicor for guarding against threats of violence by supporters of the pirates).

JUL 23 RNI closes down and Mebo II heads for Holland.

JUL 24 Broadcasting aboard Mebo II restarts, but interferes with **RADIO HILVERSUM**.

JUL 30 RNI closes down.

AUG 5 Programmes resume from 6.00 am to 3.00 pm on **RNI**.

AUG 29 An attempt is made to board Mebo II led by night-club owner **Kees Manders** aboard the tug **Viking**. He wants the Mebo II to be brought to Scheveningen, but the crew refuse, and he threatens to cut the anchor. All of the details are broadcast live on **RNI**, and appeals are made for ships in the area to come to Mebo II's rescue. Armed with knives and the burning oil from the kitchen the crew prepare to defend themselves. As this is happening, ships who have heard the appeal appear out of the mist, and **The Viking** scuttles off.

SEPT 1 CAPITAL RADIO, having sorted out some of the problems with its new ring aerial starts regular programmes. It is mainly light music and some classics. It broadcasts from 6 am to 2 am. However, further trouble arises with the aerial, and it is

DJ'S LOOKING AS POPULAR LEGEND WOULD HAVE THEM LOOK — IN THIS CASE AT *RADIO GERONIMO*

instructed to return to land. The anchors refuse to budge and have to be cut in the course of which one of the crew has his leg caught. It has later to be amputated.

SEPT 24 RNI closes down, amid reports that they had been paid to so do by **RADIO VERONICA** to the tune of one million Guilders, for the hire of the Mebo II.

OCT 8 The King David is relaunched, but on its way to the site, the aerial collapses again.

OCT 10 As **CAPITAL RADIO** begins to broadcast again, it is discovered that the ship is without her anchor. The engine has broken down, and the **King David** is drifting into shore; where she finally beaches at Noordwijk. Because of the failure of

RADIO GERONIMO to pay for the hire of the Monte Carlo transmitters, the French authorities halt further broadcasts. It remains closed.

NOV **RADIO MONTE CARLO INTERNATIONAL** comes on air, during the weekends, presented by **Tommy Vance** and **Dave Cash**, playing 'anything progressive'. The programmes are recorded in Fulham, London, and flown to Monte Carlo weekly. However poor reception problems dog the station and this results in lack of advertisers. It eventually folds.

NOV 9 At Sutton Magistrates Court 3 men are convicted of illegal broadcasts; **Nicholas Catford, David Wright** and **Howard Smith**, of **RADIO JACKIE** are ordered to pay fines of up to £50 each. The

chairman of the court, **Mr Edward Garner** says: 'You must have known your transmissions could have interfered with emergency services and spoilt the peace and enjoyment of thousands of people. If people were permitted to transmit indiscriminately we should reach a state of bedlam'.

NOV 13 The tug **Hester** tows the **King David** out to sea, and puts in a salvage bid for £11,500. The owners, **IBS** cannot afford to pay. **CAPITAL RADIO** had ceased to exist. They sign off with the following message: 'You have been listening to **CAPITAL RADIO** broadcasting on 115 kHz (270 meters) on the medium wave band. **CAPITAL RADIO** transmits with a power of 10 kw from the motor vessel **King David** anchored in international waters, **CAPITAL RADIO** is owned and operated by the world body to the broadcasting profession, the International Broadcasters Society. **CAPITAL RADIO** is dedicated to the saving of human lives and the salvation of human beings. **CAPITAL RADIO** is free radio, good radio. We hope you've enjoyed listening to us, it has been fun serving you.

89

1971

JAN 1 As **RADIO SOLENT**, the new BBC Radio Station comes on air, another station also begins to broadcast, calling itself **RADIO FREE SOLENT**.

JAN 23 Police board the 100ft converted motor torpedo boat **Eidolon** in Chichester Harbour, Sussex and discover a radio broadcast on board. Four men are taken to Ichenor to be interviewed by the Post Office investigators. The boat is placed under guard at Chester Yacht Basin after being searched by Customs officers.

FEB 20 **RNI** restarts broadcasts in English and Dutch.

MAR **RADIO VERONICA** issues a writ against **RNI** for breach of an agreement not to broadcast programmes in Dutch. Lawyers for **RNI** explain that an attempt to return the money had been made and so they were entitled to broadcast.

MAR 29 The Government's White Paper 'An Alternative Service of Broadcasting' proposes a network of about 60 commercial radio stations, under the control of a statutory body, the **Independent Broadcasting Authority**.

MAY 15 A fire is started deliberately on board **Mebo II** in the engine room. Later evidence suggests that the attempt is financed by executives of **RADIO VERONICA** who wanted to get the ship into Dutch waters. The fire stops broadcast for a few hours, but resumes, as the transmitters have not been damaged.

AUG 2 A change in scheduling of **RNI** means that Dutch programmes are now broadcast from 6.00 am to 6.00 pm, and English programmes go out from 6.00 pm to 3.00 am.

NOV 22 Mebo II broadcasts to say that she is drifting, having lost her anchor. **RNI** ceases to broadcast until she is back in international waters.

VERONICA launches a campaign of support for the station and receives more than 2,000,000 post cards from friends.

SEPT A magazine **VERONICA 192** appears to publicise the station.

THE MEBO II AT ANCHOR AND KEEPING A SHARP LOOK OUT

1972

FEB 29 Beatles Day on RADIO VERONICA results in 20 hours non stop Beatles music.

MAR 7 Phillip Whitehead, Labour MP for Derby North plays a cassette of a recording of **RADIO JACKIE** during the Committee stage of the Sound Broadcasting Bill. It is the first time that a tape recording is used during the course of a debate in Parliament.

MAR 22 Christopher Chathaway Miniter for Posts and Telecommunications tells the House of Commons that 116 people were successfully prosecuted for illegal broadcasting in the past year.

MAR 27 4.00 am: Tests are heard on 773 kHz (388 meters) for a proposed new English service for **RNI**. Over the next few weeks further tests are carried out on different frequencies: 1115 kHz (269 meters) and 845 kHz (355 meters).

MAY 29 CAROLINE NORTH is sold to **Hendrik Ido-Ambacht** at public auction, for 26,500 guilders (about £3,150). **The Fredericia** was then broken up for scrap.

MAY 29 The Mi Amigo, home of **CAROLINE SOUTH** is sold to **Hofmmann Shipping**, £2,400 (20,000 Guilders). It is

assumed she will be broken up.

JUN 11 The Rev. James Paterson, a Minister at Palmers Green Elim Pentecostal church is charged with operating a transmitter without a licence. **RADIO ODYSSEY** played 'hot gospel' music throughout North London.

SEPT 3 Mi Amigo drops anchor off Scheveningen.

SEPT 29 Non stop music on 1187kHz (253 meters) is noted from the **Mi Amigo**. Erratic test broadcasts continue for the next few weeks.

SEPT 30 VERONICA moves frequency to 538 meters and leaves a low power broadcast on the old 192 slot, advising listeners of the change. The final programme on 192 is a half hour history of the station and then presenter **Tineke** says: 'We hope to see you on the 538 spot'. The time is 12.30 pm. At 1.00 pm on 538 normal programmes resume. At 12.30 pm **Tony Allen** comes on air on 1562 kHz (192 meters): 'Good afternoon ladies and gentlemen, this is the start of test transmissions from **RNI 2**'. But apart from an occasional broadcast, very infrequent up to the beginning of Oct, nothing more is heard.

> **"I think we have to seriously consider the enormous disadvantages of having a vast army of people who can communicate with one another very easily . . ."**
>
> LORD WELLS-PESTEL
> of The Home Office

OCT 8 London's first IBA franchised station, **LONDON BROADCASTING** comes on air. **RADIO LUXEMBOURG**, puts an ad in the daily papers, saying: 'Owing to an oversight commercial radio will not be starting in October' and claims that it is 'Britain's one and only national commercial radio station'.

OCT 24 English broadcasts cease on **RNI**. This happens on the orders of the Dutch director of programmes, who announces that he is sacking the English staff.

NOV 3 The Swiss owners of **RNI** overrule the decision of the Dutch director, and reinstates English broadcasts.

NOV 13 Force eleven gale pulls the **Mi Amigo** off her anchor and demolishes the mast. A makeshift repair is carried out.

DEC 28 Erratic business from the **Mi Amigo**. Unpaid crew cut the fuel line to the generator and leave the ship. 3.40pm: **Andy Archer** reports strange visitors on deck and interrupts his show to check. It is the Dutch Royal Navy with a tender containing the recently departed crew. Fighting breaks out.

DEC 30 The Mi Amigo is towed to Ijmuiden under the control of Captain **van der Kamp**. The complaints and seizure reportedly due to unpaid bills.

91

DUNCAN JOHNSON

VARIOUS (CANADA/W.INDIES)
RADIO LONDON
RADIO NORDZEE INTERNATIONAL

RADIO ONE
CAPITAL RADIO (IBA)
INVICTA SOUND (ILR)

Duncan Johnson came to offshore radio as an experienced broadcaster, one of the recruits from Canada that gave *Radio* London the edge over other pirate stations. For Johnson it was a deliberate career progression . . .

"I originated from near Toronto, I left school when I was 15 to be an apprentice printer and I did that for a year. I didn't think very kindly of it so I was an itinerant odd job man for the next couple of years travelling around Western Canada, then I met up with and was working with a friend whose father owned a big ranch. He had left home because he didn't want to work on the farm; we were working together in Calgary, Alberta, he said he was going home to start at the local radio station, because we had talked about it — getting a job in radio."

He went into his local radio station and they said they needed somebody to do the farm reports, he told them that the reason he wanted the job in radio was to get away from a farm, and they said 'you can have that job and we'll let you play records on a Sunday night if you like' so he did.

Meantime I was still working and I went to see him in autumn and his boss asked me what I knew about radio and I said 'this is the first time I have ever been in a radio station'; and he said 'we can't give you a job, you don't know anything about it. If you go to a place called Swift-current, Saskatchawan, you'll get a job there because they will hire anyone'.

So I got on the Greyhound bus and went off to Swift-current, and I asked for a job, and they said 'why should ve give you one', I said 'because I want one', so they said ok, when can you start'.

That was October 1960 and it was a disastrous place, tiny, sitting on the world's second largest helium deposit which was of no value because it was too deep and nobody wanted helium in those days, now they are probably all millionaires.

The guy who had sent me there phoned and said 'would you like a job', I said 'yes'. He said 'I haven't told you what the job is yet', and I said 'I'll take it'. I went back to Lesbridge, Alberta, in the foothills of the mountains, and I was doing a little bit of everything there, late nights, five hours and six hours on a Saturday night doing Top 40 stuff, which even in those days was out of my line. Running a record library as well. When one of the blokes from Swiftcurrent got a job in Bermuda, we were doing tape letters back and forth; one New Years Day after I had been at Lesbridge for nearly a year, I sent a tape letter saying, 'there must be something in Bermuda, it must be warmer than this', and his boss said 'does he want a job'.

So I was in Bermuda for 18 months and we all decided to come over here because radio was going to start, unfortunately *pirate* radio wasn't ready to start because that was 1963.''

Johnson applied to join *Radio London* **and had the advantage of a professional audition tape and some real experience. He found himself one of the senior men aboard the** *Galaxy* **launching what was to enter history as pirate radio . . .**

'I was just around, I was doing all sorts of things, extras in movies, working in pubs and all sorts of things and I read about *Radio London.* I knew *Caroline* had started, because they started in the summer of '64. Then I read in the Daily Mail, **Dougie Marlborough** wrote the story of this new pirate station starting. I got hold of him and he told me where he had got the story from, which was some PR people. They gave me the name of **Philip Birch** who then said 'you want to talk to **Ben Tony** who is the man in charge of doing all that', so I went to see him. All I had was a small reel of tape with three commercials on it, which I had recorded 18 months earlier in Bermuda. He said to me 'we're not ready to start it yet, I'll bear you in mind', that was in November.

I was working on a movie, and we worked through Christmas and January, come the end of January and I hadn't heard anything from him, we had been on a big party for the end of this movie, I got up in the morning with a bit of a hang over and phoned up Ben Tony and he said 'I want you to be here at 12' and I said 'I could make it 12.30' and he said 'no I've got a lunch appointment', and I said 'o.k. quarter past 12'. I put on a suit and tie and went down to the office in Curzon Street and he said 'wait in here for me' and two minutes later Philip Birch came in and said 'oh, you're the new man that is starting are you? Nice to see a clean cut one with a suit and tie' That is how I got the job.

I said 'how do I get there'. He said 'if you go to Ipswich, to the Shipping Agent there and they will put you on the boat'. I went to Ipswich, this being the first day of February and the Shipping Agent said 'our Contract ended the end of January, they are now in Harwich' I said 'who are *they*' and he said 'I don't know the agents name but that is where they are'.

Radio London was alright, it was *Caroline* they were all very wary of. I then had to get to Harwich, Parkstone Quay, it started snowing, I didn't know where I was going.

I got a cab and said 'Parkstone Quay', and the guy said 'are you one of those radio people' and I said 'I might be', and he said 'I know where you want to go then, I took **Simon Dee** there yesterday'. He took me to the Shipping Agent and they said they were the new ones for *Radio London*: 'but we haven't got you on our list, we don't know anything about you, besides the boat has already gone out, but it is going again at 6 o'clock tonight'. I hung around and nobody on board the ship knew I was arriving but eventually got there about 7 o'clock that night completely befuddled by the whole thing.

The weather was getting rough then, and it got extremely rough, the first three days I would have got off if I could have done, it was that sort of thing, but there was no way because the tender couldn't get alongside, but after that I just got used to it. I said to the Captain, 'I want a life jacket' and this little Captain who was on said 'don't give me a hard time, come up to the wheelhouse', and it was going back and forth, side to side and he said 'see that meter it is going 25° that way isn't it', I said 'that's right' and he said 'now watch it, it only goes 15° the other way, we won't tip over like that it has to go 25° both ways before it will tip, besides there aren't enough lifejackets on here'.''

The station quickly became known as the number one professional station with it's tight programming and Americanised sound. It's aims different to those of *Radio Caroline,* **a near neighbour . . .**

''It was pretty tight, except for **Kenny Everett**, Ben Tony would set up a format and we had to stick to the format, he used to come out once a week and do the play list, the Top 40 and whatever, and it was rotated, except we had an album track we could play each hour if we wanted and that was a free choice.

The oldies — we had great reels of oldies that had come over from America on this big machine and they just went in rotation, some of them used to skip out one or two now and again, because some of them had never been heard of.

The first six months were a bit difficult because the transmitter would not work properly and the generator wasn't operating properly.

They thought of the idea of having a mine sweeper with this enormous great generator, for the electro magnet field which fended off mines, and they thought they could make use of this generator but it just reverberated throughout the whole boat, the whole thing was going and it was too much power to run the transmitter.

It was very spartan in the early days, the equipment they bought was good and new, except we didn't have any blankets, they had taken all the blankets down into the hold and they had made walls to soundproof the studios. But the equipment was new and that was one decided advantage over the others, and the transmitter was good, it was just a question of getting it to work at sea.

We were never short of money. I went on having my three weeks on, because we were told we would do two weeks on and one week off, but because it was the beginning we weren't actually on the air. I had stayed on three weeks to get the rotas right because I was the eighth one at that time, and then we came off and the Shipping Agent signed a piece of paper and he gave me the cash and he said 'I do apologise, I've run out of fivers, would one pound notes be o.k.'. He proceeded to count out in 30 one pound notes, which was quite good money, certainly enough to get me a large brandy in the Railway Bar immediately after that.

But we never ever had any problem with money, we knew the other pirate ships did, they weren't funded like us, they were funded by locals whereas this one had all come from America.''

There were rumours aplenty of the source of funding for the radio station and in the climate of the day politics and pop music were an inflammatory combination. The President of the United States, Lyndon Johnson, was reputed to be involved with the station indirectly through his wife Ladybird, a fact that could endear Radio London **to the Government of the day.**

"The only thing that can be said is that the man who was our boss, who we were told was the big man, also had shares in the television station in America which **Ladybird Johnson** had shares in, or it was meant to be her station. They had some investments together and whether that amounted to her investing in Radio London I don't know.

We didn't realise the impact we were making initially, because we kept thinking, 'is there anybody out there'. We weren't getting any reaction from record companies, which in many ways was understandable because they had decided we were illegal and we were cutting into their programming on Luxembourg. At that time they all bought their programmes in Luxembourg and they had to play one third of the record just to get the people at it a little bit, just as a teaser so they would want to hear what the rest of the record was like. That was the theory behind those type of Radio Luxembourg programmes, and it wasn't until people like **Kit Lambert** with the Who got started. He was probably the instrumental one, the one that I remember most anyway, because he came round and had done a deal through Decca. People were asking for Who records in the shops because we were playing it on London and and

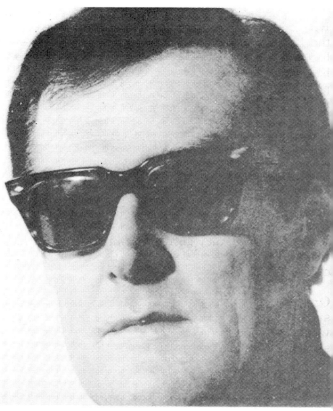

TONY WINDSOR A SEMINAL FIGURE AND HERO IN RADIO BROADCASTING

couldn't get it.

I even remember seeing the back seat of his car loaded up with records saying 'I can't stop and chat now I've got to take these around to the shops, Decca just won't supply the record shops, I had to go collect them myself and then go and deliver'.

That was just what was happening with Radio London, the impact it was going to have and he said 'it's only because London is playing the record, there is no call for it anywhere else in the country, it is all in the South East, you have made a market for it and it is going to get big.'

By the time we got through that Summer, it was June when we were still breaking down occasionally, by that Summer of '65 end of July, it was there. They were all lining up on beaches and flashing lights and doing the whole works and it just went on from there, got bigger and bigger, and the money started coming in more.''

The fact that Johnson and the other jocks on London **were older kept them out of the essentially youthful extramural activities of being a pirate radio presenter. Their experience got them more involved with the business development of the company rather than the social life.**

"I never did any roadshows. We used to have to go to the Marquee on Saturday; some of them used to go round, but there weren't quite so many disco shows in those days as there are now.

On *London,* **Tony Windsor**, **Paul Kay**, and **Earl Richmond** weren't really the type of people to dive into the disco, we were older and except for **Kenny Everett** had all had some experience with radio. **Dave Dennis** hadn't had a lot, he had worked on some of the other pirates for a while but the rest of us had all worked in Australian or North American radios of some kind.

As far as the radio went we were very close although not personal friends. That worked on the ship, but we were *Radio London* and we didn't have a lot to do with the other ones, although we knew them and said hello and had to travel on the same tender at times. It wasn't part of a pirate radio, we never considered ourselves as a mysterious pirate radio organisation we were a broadcasting company, a radio station.

Even today they go round with these pirate radio conventions and things, we were never really part of that, certainly not the early mob of us."

Once the business of offshore radio was in full swing the financiers of the various operations were keen to expand. The successful ship owners soon cast a speculative eye over the various forts dotted around the Thames Estuary, mostly in the hands of small time local amateurs with cash problems...

"We went out with an engineer **Martin Newton** and **Dennis Maitland** who was *London's* Office Manager, the four of us went with **Reg Calvert**. We were going to see this fort of his and take it over and put on another extension to *Radio London.*

We were travelling down the M2 and he said 'we've had a bit of bother in the past, but I've got one of these things' and he pulled out this little pen and said 'they are gas guns, nobody bothers you with those, you give them a squirt of that in the eyes and it is knock out'.

He talked about these other things and these hair brain schemes he was doing and how he was going to use a low frequency transmitter by sticking a copper tube down into the sea and send low frequency signals down through the water which would then come out all over the place and expand. I thought the guy is mad, he lived up in Warwickshire somewhere near the BBC transmitter sites and he used to send balloons up on a copper cable to interfere with their broadcasts and tried to send out his own.

He was a nut case, the only thing good about him was he used to manage **Screaming Lord Sutch** who I thought was a likeable nutcase

Shivering Sands Fort is what it was called, because Sutch had been on that one; because I had met him in 1964 and he wanted me to come out on his fort and read lines from *Lady Chatterleys Lover* because there was a court case on at the moment as to whether it was pornographic. He said 'you've got just the right voice, you could do that for me couldn't you', and I said 'how do I get out there' and when he told me I said 'no, I don't think so'.

Nevertheless, here we were with Calvert. We were

offered the choice of going up this little 1″ cable hoist and he said 'that is how everybody goes up' and I said 'bugger that, I'm not going up there', and **Keith Skues** said the same and so we crawled up the ladder.

Then when we got to the top where there should have been steps and things, it was scaffolding rails which were a bit loose and some of the metal steps were a bit rotted away, and I said to Skues 'are you still with me', and he said 'yes'. I said 'I don't know how we are going to get down again, but here we go', we started up, and looking up you could see this vision in blue, pale blue jeans, blue jumper and blue hat and he said 'Hello, my name is **Tom Edwards**, but everyone on here calls me mother'... and I promptly stepped back into Skues' hand. He nearly fell off the ladder into the sea. We had a look round this place and it was some little old turntable he had found somewhere, it still had kickback when the turntable arm re-set itself, and it was all home-made equipment on there and it looked like a doss house compared to *Radio London.*"

RADIO CITY, THE SOURCE OF MUCH TRAGEDY

The *Radio London* team were not the only ones to think that the forts and towers would be a superior base for a transmitter if they were properly converted. Ronan O'Rahilly was pursuing a similar line of inquiry. *Radio City*, however, was a long way from being properly constituted. It was a serious turn of events that defeated many of the plans to develop the ex-military structures for broadcasting. And the chance would never occur again . . .

"There was a big enough room for a transmitter, all these separate rooms and they needed to put a couple of new walkways through. So we had decided where the studio would have gone and where the transmitter would have gone.

The transmitter tower was already there. Reg Calvert didn't use the tower because the cable blew down one day and it just hung out the window of the fort then, he found he got a better signal in central London with the cable hanging out of the window than up the tower, so he just used the tower for his television aerial.

It probably would have done, it wasn't entirely safe because one section of it had fallen down and the section was standing all on its own with the walkways down on it, but it was fairly sound the bit of it that was standing.

We didn't know anything about the dispute between Reg Calvert and this other bloke **Oliver Smedley**, we were down on the Embankment near the White Elephant and it was a big night, all the press had been invited and it was going to be the opening night, with the official launch of *Radio London* taking over and they were going to record a programme and it was going to be the start. Then suddenly all these heavy news journalists started showing up and we didn't know what the bloody hell was going on, suddenly they all disappeared.

It wasn't until the next morning we heard that Smedley had shot Reg Calvert and there was half page photograph in the Daily Mail of Keith Skues, myself, Martin Newton the engineer and Dennis Maitland standing on this little boat going out to the *Radio City* fort.

THE MEBO II, THE PSYCHEDELIC PIRATE AT ANCHOR

This was the *Radio London* team going out and we didn't know why the shooting was being done, so we had to go into hiding ourselves."

Johnson left the ship around the same time. The Marine Offences Act was looming, although as a Canadian he would be immune from a jail sentence, getting into the country may have proved difficult. The owners of *Radio London* were not interested in breaking the law however . . .

"They weren't bothered by the whole thing, they were just interested in running the radio station.

I went back onto the *London* ship in July and August for holiday relief, but they had already hired more people to replace us, it is just one of those things that didn't work out having made the move away — to try and work again, and in that kind of business it is all so new and changes so much, you can't go back and retrace your steps.

In the last six months there was a quick turnover of staff because I think *Radio London* knew that the MOA was unavoidable and that they weren't going to carry on the way *Caroline* did, trying to scrape a living doing it, if they couldn't run it properly, they weren't going to do it."

Duncan Johnson worked briefly with the pirate ship *Radio North Sea International,* of all the offshore broadcasters it was *RNI* that lived up to the name of pirate.

"It all started with **Roger Day**, through him and a guy **Rodney Collins** who used to work for the Record Mirror, got involved in *Radio North Sea*. He came to me one day and said would I go out onto *Radio North Sea*, and I said I would like to go up and have a look round. I don't think I was working, I had a photographic studio and I had just sold my share in it to my partner, so I wasn't doing anything. I had just bought a house, I went out there for the first fortnight, I don't remember doing any broadcasting, but some people said I did. I had three fortnights on there that was all.

It was on the English coast and we had to travel across in this terrible boat, I did get sea sick on that one, that was the only time I was ever really seasick.

We didn't really know who these Swiss people were, I never met them until the last fortnight that I was on there and when they came on they said they were doing this and that. Then they said they had millions of pounds to do this and that. I said 'what about the £50 you promised me' and they said 'I'm not sure whether we can do that'. I thought, it's all very well to talk about millions of pounds.

This was *Mebo II* because the first boat was too small, they used it to go back and forth across the Channel."

Johnson was one of the DJ's who the BBC thought it natural to give a try for *Radio 1*, it was to prove less than a success for him there, although the BBC were themselves thrashing around trying get the formula right for the fledgling station.

"I got to know quite a few of the people at *Radio 1*, **Johnny**

Berling and a lot of the *Radio 1* producers. I had done a few bits and pieces for them for the Home Service before *Radio 1* started.

They obviously decided, the powers that be at *Radio 1*, who said get all these names, all the ones that are acceptable, and lets get them on and start our own station and we'll sort them out when we get to it. So of course they hired everybody. **Ed Stewart** was the first one to go although he got back again and I was the second one. Then they cleared them all out fairly quickly after that except for the obvious two or three who made it.

The *Radio London* outfit was another radio station, not a pirate, not a thing in the night. It was good and solid and became part of the establishment, then it was time to move on with the establishment and my only problem with the BBC was it was too great a change, it was too much establishment for me. I didn't understand the way the establishment worked, which I would do now, but I couldn't fit into the confines of each thing being documented.

They tried to make it free and easy. *Radio 1* started off being made to sound that way, but it was even more restricted than some people imagine it, although it didn't always sound that way on the air; it sounded free and easy. But there were still a lot of people in the BBC who objected to setting up a 'pop' station, and the conflicts within the BBC itself reverberated through *Radio 1*, and for those that managed to stay they had stamina and could follow it through."

DUNCAN JOHNSON ABOUT TO JOIN *INVICTA SOUND*

Johnson shares with many of the more experienced presenters a retrospective view of the pirate phenomena that steers well clear of the romantic. It's a view most of the non-British jocks seem to hold, maybe because they had not been brought up under the BBC monopoly and with Workers Playtime . . .

"It was nothing more than just a business as far as we were concerned.

It was a phase in the life of the country as much as a phase in the life of an individual, because it was instrumental in changing the way the music and entertainment business operates in this country.

I think we were all pleased to be there and to be instrumental in that change because we knew that it would have to come, that it just couldn't stay cocooned away for that amount of time, things were going to happen. What we didn't foresee was that it would take so long for it to happen and it hasn't really happened the way we anticipated.

The IBA insists that a local station be all things to all people and I find it is just an impossibility. You have to segment your talent and your market and your audience, and try to be the best for that share of your audience that you can, do the best possible thing you can and that is where the IBA are slowly coming around. Because they know it is not a commercially viable thing to be all things to all people. As for the other little pirate stations that are around I don't understand them because they are anarchistic, they are not a viable commercial proposition because that is what a commerical radio should be. They say they are operating that way but won't pay any royalties, *Capital Radio* has to pay about 20% of advertising revenue in royalties, and there is no way that these stations could afford to carry on like that.

Laser is a completely different kettle of fish to the local pirates. I don't understand who it is that is financing *Laser* and why they are putting so much money into them. It is illegal in Europe to advertise on these stations, so I can't see where there is going to be a big enough market to warrant them continuing to run an expensive operation."

Johnson has just moved from his slot on London's *Capital Radio* **to Canterbury's ILR station** *Invicta Sound*. **a position, he freely admits, partly due to the influence that** *Laser* **has had on most commercial stations within it's scope. Essex radio stations are reputed to have lost as much as 30% of their audience to the American radio ship.**

"The way things are going at *Capital* it may not last that much longer. I'm stuck between two doors at present, *Capital* is changing. I'm interested in selling the advertising as well, which is a natural step in North American or Australian radio. They say: sell yourselves on the air as a presenter and then go out and sell the Radio Station. Work your way through and build a career in local radio as opposed to a career as a broadcaster or presenter. There are only so many personalities.

1973

JAN 15 Test broadcasts by the IBA in London for **CAPITAL RADIO** blot out **RADIO VERONICA** for most of England (and Belgium). **RADIO VERONICA** threatens to swamp the medium waveband 206 meters if the IBA fail to stop the tests.

FEB Bad weather forces **RADIO VERONICA** to go out live due to no fresh tapes being supplied.

FEB 23 A broken anchor forces **RNI** to stop transmission as the **Mebo II** heads towards the Dutch coast. It resumes transmissions the following day.

APR 2/3 North Sea experiences the worst weather in living memory. A hurricane devastates the **Norderney RADIO VERONICA** radio ship and she calls Scheveningen Radio at 8.45 pm to say she is lose and drifting towards shore. The lifeboat **Bernard van Leer** puts out to sea to effect a rescue, she takes off four men. Shortly after the life boat takes off the remaining six men. By 11.30pm the **Norderney** is aground fifty yards from the entrance to Schevenigen Harbour. Such is the weather that the lifeboat cannot enter the harbour at all until 10 am the next day. **RNI** is also affected by storms, forcing the station to close.

APR 4 Offers of help come from **RNI** and **CAROLINE**. The Dutch version of **RADIO 1, HILVERSUM III**, schedule a broadcast from the stranded ship and lay cable from Scheveningen Radio buildings. It is cancelled at the last minute.

APR 7 6.00 am: The salvage crew fail to refloat the **Norderney**. The same happens the following day. The tug **Smitband** also fails to tow her off the beach.

APR 11 Using the **Mi Amigo** at cost price, a gift from **Ronan O'Rahilly**, **RADIO VERONICA** recommences broadcasting on 253 meters, regular programmes by noon.

APR 18 4.00 am: The **Norderney** is refloated and by 5am is back at anchor. By 10 am the station is back on air. The **Mi Amigo** broadcasts details of the return until 11 am and then for two days relays the programmes.

APR 24 The damage done by storm to the FM antenna of **RNI** is repaired and broadcasting commences again.

MAY 16 MV Peace sets off from New York. The Radio station aboard **THE VOICE OF PEACE** broadcasts its first tests on 1540 kHz (195 meters). Its destination is the Coast of Israel. The MV Peace is a 570 ton freighter, formerly MV **Cito** 170 foot in length. It is owned by **Abraham S. Nathan**, whose aim is to provide a place where Jews and Arabs can publicise their views.

MAY 26 Programmes start from **VOICE OF PEACE** mainly in English, but also in French, Hebrew and Arabic. In the main the station operates from noon to 2.00 am.

JUL 15 **RADIO ATLANTIS** opens. It is broadcast from the **Mi Amigo** where wealthy Belgian businessman **Adriaan van Lanschoot** hires one of the transmitters.

THE OCEANIC, HOME OF *RADIO FREE AMERICA* OWNED BY THE REV CARL McINTIRE

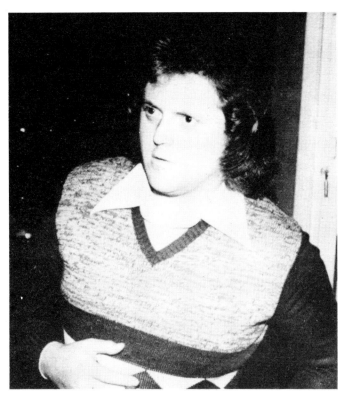

ABOVE: ADRIAAN VAN LANDSCHOOT ON THE LOSING SIDE OF A DEAL OVER A TELESCOPIC MAST — O'RAHILLY WINS THE DAY

It is in Flemish. The programmes are pre-recorded and broadcast between 6 am and 7 pm. This method is to result in the station being off the air several times when new tapes cannot be delivered because of bad weather. Old tapes have to be repeated.

SEPT 13 RFA (RADIO FREE AMERICA) commences with a test. This lasts for a half hour before transmitter trouble stops the test. The station is aboard the motor vessel **Columbus** (formerly Oceanic). It is owned by the **Rev. Carl McIntire**. It transmits on 1160 kHz (259 meters). It is anchored off Cape May, New Jersey.

SEPT 14 Columbus loses its anchor, and has to return to port.

SEPT 19 RFA begins regular transmissions. It starts with a

hymn followed by **Rev. McIntire**. It soon attracts complaints from local stations, especially from WHLW in Lakewood N.J. (on 70 kHz). **Rev McIntire** stops transmitting.

SEPT 20 At Camden, N.J. a federal judge restrains RFA from further broadcasts.

SEPT 23 Apart from a brief test on a different frequency 1608 kHm (186 meters), RFA ceases to exist, admidst a legal wrangle.

OCT 16 Capital Radio, opens as a middle-of-the-road station serving Greater London, on 539 meters (95.8 FM stereo)

OCT 17 An Israeli gunboat comes alongside **Peace** and orders it to shore. THE VOICE OF PEACE has been appealing to the soldiers to lay down their arms.

OCT 18 RADIO ATLANTIS goes off the air.

OCT 31 Adriaan van Lanschoot buys the Zandaxonagen, to relaunch RADIO ATLANTIS, for 50,000 Guilders (about £8000). **van Lanschoot** renames the ship Jeanine, after his wife. The Zondaxanogon had been the base for an ill-fated attempt to launch RADIO CONDOR. The ship is an ex-Icelandic trawler **Emma**. Its engines have previously been destroyed by fire.

NOV 3 Test transmissions begin from aboard the **Jeanine**, on a number of frequencies.

NOV 6 Jeanine is found drifting, abandoned a mile from the Dutch coast. The tug **Titan** tows her to Cuxhaven in Germany. She is refurbished.

NOV 9 THE VOICE OF PEACE, having failed to find backers, finally goes off the air.

NOV 11 RNI extends its broadcasts to become a 24 hour station.

NOV 13 Storms put VERONICA off the air for three hours. Some programmes consist of non-stop music when tapes failed to be delivered. The oil crisis is on and the 24 hour weekend service is cancelled. It is planned to cease transmitting after midnight in December.

DEC 22 Jeanine is towed from Cuxhaven to a position of Knocke in Belgium.

DEC 23 RADIO ATLANTIS begins test transmission on 115 kHz (269 meters). But problems continue to dog the transmissions, as the equipment is still incomplete.

DEC 24 RADIO MILINDA is forced off the air after a police raid on a Dublin flat. It has operated for the last eighteen months, and was run by a group of young volunteers with a mixture of music and local news.

DEC 30 By this time RADIO ATLANTIS is broadcasting in Flemish (6am-7pm) and English (7pm-6am). But again transmitter failure puts the station off the air.

media zoot

It has got to be admitted that **Richard Branson** has shown a lot of courage with his magazine *Event*. After a dubious start, hampered by the design of **Pearce Marchbank** (i.e. un-readable), the typesize was increased to make it more legible to normal human beings and the magazine settled down. A cleverly stage-managed bluff regarding a *Private Eye* scandal got *Event* a mass of publicity which was, on the basis of the story, quite undeserved. Of course, the 'revelations' that most of the contributors to the *Eye* were pals of its editor; were Fleet Street 'names' themselves; spent time dallying with each others wives and would suppress a story to protect their jobs, is nothing new. There can't be an editor in the country, including Branson, that wouldn't kill a report if it suits him and this naturally applies to **Richard Ingrams**. The only notable thing about the *Eye* story was (a) its none credited author, and (b) it was one of the few anti-*Eye* stories ever to be printed since the Ingrams team became looked on as journalistic Robin Hoods. The former is no real mystery. The picture was made up of an amalgam of information from various sources (of which the initials T.S. could play an important role) and cobbled together in a bland style devoid of any personal stamp. It is a fact that most columnists reveal themselves by the pace of their syntax. As for the latter, Most punters love a 'look behind the scenes' and care little for accuracy - it doesn't matter if Lord X dresses in women's clothes, it's the thought that counts. Mugs will still contribute to the various 'Balls' funds - a brilliant money raising idea if ever there was one! But back to *Event*. After this massive plug for their intelligence service, *Event* had to follow it up the next week. By now *Event* was into issue 4 and the cracks were beginning to appear, nothing much - less pages despite an increased typesize here

and there, and the **Chinese Whispers** of which they seemed so proud dissolved into the realms of fantasy. Writing a weekly gossip-based column is not the easiest thing in the world. Despite massive slush funds and years at it, look what Fleet Street comes up with? Trash! The rules are simple and based on the Lord X mentality - innuendo and lies are OK if you can't be sued (Royal Family stuff) or checked up on (deceased or Government 'secrets'). **Chinese Whispers** favour both. **Example:**

Tainted money reminds me of the fate of that pirate radio station, **Nordzee**, which the governments around the North Sea went to such trouble to jam. It's real offence was not the harmless rock it relayed over the water, but the amount of expensive listening devices that it positioned under them.

Just right for listening to the NATO submarines in action, of course. And where did Radio Nordzee get most of its money from? Points east of the Oder-Niesse line, so NATO discovered. Hard luck Nordzee fans. Didn't know you were listening to the voice of the Soviets, did you? . . .

Event Issue 4

It would be difficult to think of a more fatuous story than this. Electronics experts would be interested to learn from *Event* how you go about *jamming* a free ranging *listening* device? So would the two young Swiss engineers **Meister** and **Bollier** whose life dream was the return of 'pirate radios'. In Easter 1969 they finally committed themselves to that dream, bought a Norwegian coaster called it **MEBO I**. Fitting out began right away and they found to their dismay that the boat was too small! (Well, the **KGB** are inefficient!) Shortly after they acquired the *Silvretta*, a freighter much the same size as the famous sixties 'pirates'. Refitted in

Rotterdam to bring the total investment up to 4 million Swiss Francs (God knows how many roubles), by late January 1970, the 22nd to be precise, the **MEBO 2** dropped anchor 52°21′1″ Northern Latitude, 4°18′5″ Eastern Longitude - 3 miles outside Noordwijk. Despite gales of 7 to 9 the engineers were ready to make the first FM test transmissions the following day. The first live show hit the air wave on the 28th of February to a mass of international press, radio and TV coverage. Amongst the D.Js were British 'Soviet agents' **Roger Day** and **Andy Archer**. Fan letters arrived by the van load. By March 1970 they moved to a position 3 miles off Clacton and broadcast first on 186m and then 190m wave band. From the moment the **MEBO 2** came within British P.T. range the jamming of *broadcasts* began - the government in the '70s was very sensitive to the pirate radio cult having successfully crushed it only a short time before.

Nordzee returned returned to the Dutch coast but immediately ran into competition with the long-established *Radio Veronica*. After notice from the Dutch government they altered frequency away from 224m to 220m. There followed a series of high jinx - night club owner **Kees Mandes** tried to board and pirate the pirate, all reported live over the air. **Nordzee** was saved by a Royal Netherlands frigate *Van Nees* amongst others. **Nordzee** came off the air first in October 1970. The reason - finance, plain and simple. Bankruptcy loomed to the tune of millions although the ship remained at anchor off the Dutch coast. In the end they struck a deal with *Veronica* who more or less paid them to be off the air. When this charter aggreement finished Meister and Bollier decided to give the project one last spin. Unfortunately this alienated the *Veronica* organisation once and for all time. In February 1971 the station broadcast several hours

of none stop music. Ashore, in liason with the Dutch firm **Basart**, Mebo Ltd founded the *N.V. Exploitatie Maatschappij Radio Nordzee* to sell air time to advertisers. In February two english soviet agent D.J.s **Alan West** and **Steve Marike** boosted by two Dutch guys (the publicity people wanted programmes in Dutch) started test broadcasts. Despite a slur campaign by new adversaries *Radio Veronica*, all went well until the 15th of May 1971. The english speaking show was interrupted by MAYDAY calls and the **MEBO 2** was on fire - the result of an incendiary bomb planted by frogmen. Not SAS unfortunately but 3 men were subsequently arrested and admitted to working for a rival station. In consequence the *Radio Veronica* directors were arrested. However, all the excitement became too much for the Dutch who ratified the 'Anti Pirate Law' and in the end **Nordzee** became a victim of the newly international Marine Offences Act. And that was that.

Technical Note: Most Western and Eastern Bloc powers monitor submarine movement by two methods. Satellite - or more cheaply by autonomous detectors that sit in networks on the ocean bed. Dropped by trawlers, subs, navy ships or spy ships they resemble the motorway flashing amber lights mounted on tripods, and form a sea bed 'listening grid'. Developed for detection purposes under the polar ice caps their strength is that they are un-manned, un-marked, activated by sound otherwise dormant and relatively cheap. They are nothing new.

SHARP REBUFF

It is a pity that **Tony Elliott** at *Time Out* felt the need to retaliate to the *Private Eye* non story. He used ex-wife **Janet Street-Porter** to do it. Maybe it was a last minute rush, but all the thinking mans belisha beacon could come up with was a page on how she was in with the 'in' crowd and thus knew the story already!(?) The relevance of this was lost on most people although it may take the pressure off **Jennifer Sharp**, who rarely enters the thoughts of a thinking man, although she does know a couple. Poor Ms Sharp was telephonically abused by **Nigel Dempster** as being the author of the piece and especially the items that slighted people like herself. It would be a minor league and would not have the bottle to slit her own throat so early in an aspiring career. She knows full well that secret sources have a habit of being revealed only too flatulently.

WILD ACCUSATIONS EVEN MADE THE SMALL PRESS. A PAGE FROM THE 'CHELSEA SET' MAGAZINE: NEW STYLE 1980

JAN 7 Transmissions restart from **RADIO ATLANTIS**, but even now the problems with the transmitters have not been solved. Over the next few weeks a variety of frequencies are to be used.

APR 4 Jamming from Eastern Europe interfers with **RADIO ATLANTIS** and causes it to move frequencies yet again. Troubles still beset equipment, causing breaks in transmissions.

JUN 6 A storm causes the aerial aboard **Jeanine** to collapse, and **RADIO ATLANTIS** goes off the air. There is further trouble with the transmitter.

JUN 7 The storm continues overnight and when the crew wake up they find they have lost their anchor, and have drifted into land at Westkapelle.

JUN 8 **Jeanine** is towed back to Knokke.

JUN 9 **RADIO ATLANTIS** restarts broadcasts.

JUN 10 The newly installed linear amplifier blows causing a fire aboard **RADIO ATLANTIS**.

AUG 17 D.J. **Steve England** announces that **RADIO ATLANTIS** is to comply with the Dutch Marine Offences Act,

and close.

AUG 30 The **RADIO ATLANTIS** DJ's all broadcast their farewell shows.
Brian Banks is sentenced to six months and **Ronald Cand** to 3 months for illegal broadcasts from **RADIO PENELOPE** on equipment which had been stolen.

AUG 31 6 pm: **RADIO VERONICA** is to comply with Dutch Marine Broadcasting Act. From 5 pm DJ **Rob Out** presents his show with a clock ticking ominously in the background. After the 5.30 pm news **Bull Verweij** says farewell via a pre-recorded tape and at 6 pm the station dies with these words from **Rob Out** 'This is the end of **VERONICA**, it's a pity for you, for **VERONICA** and especially democracy in Holland.' The Dutch National Anthem is followed by a jingle which goes dead half way through. The staff arrive in Schevenigen to be met by a large crowd of supporters.

6.00 pm: The Goodbye Show' is broadcast on **RADIO ATLANTIS**. It then closes down.

RNI ceases broadcasts at 8 pm when the Dutch and English DJ and the management says their farewells and the signature tune of RNI is played.

SEPT 1 The Marine Offices Act becomes law in Holland.

SEPT 9 The Mebo II arrives in Slikkerveer, to undergo a complete overhaul, and to upgrade the transmitters and studio equipment aboard. Rumours circulate that it is to be relaunched under the name of **RADIO NOVA INTERNATIONAL**, broadcasting off the coast of Italy.

OCT 10 Mebo II is seized by Dutch authorities.

OCT 11 A preliminary hearing is held to determine the status of **Mebo II**. Dutch

law prevents any ship from carrying a transmitter for a purpose other than maritime communications.

NOV 29 At the High Court in Brussels **Adriaan van Landschoot** is found guilty of offences against the **Belgian Marine Offices Act 1962**. He is fined 1 ½ million francs (£18,000) and three other directors are fined 300,000 francs (£3,500) each.

DEC 10 Mebo II is allowed to leave, as the Panamanian consul had stated that the ship was registered in Panama.

FEB 20 Four men, a furniture maker, a labourer, a storekeeper and one unemployed are convicted of operating an illegal station, **ANGLIA FREE COMMERCIAL RADIO** from a wood near Cambridge. Cambridge Magistrates Court order the men to pay fines ranging from £50 to £70, and their transmitter is confiscated.

MAR 27 After further protracted wrangling, **Mebo II** is finally allowed to leave, subject to an agreement that it would not broadcast from water anywhere in Europe for two years. It has to pay a surety of 250,000 Guilders (£44,000).

NOV 14 A combined Home Office Navy and police operation is launched against the **Mi Amigo** 20 miles off Walton-on-the-Naze. The police also apprehend two men in a small boat, taken by police launch to Southend and charged under the **Marine Offences Act**.

DEC 11 Three men are committed for trial on charges of conspiracy together and with others to install wireless telegraphy equipment on the Gunfleet Old Lighthouse knowing that their broadcasts were to be made from there. It is the first time the conspiracy section of the 1967 **M.O.A.** is used.

1976

APR 1 RADIO ONE'S programmes are hi-jacked for half an hour by pirates. A powerful portable transmitter is sited near the BBC's unmanned transmitter at Rowridge, Isle of Wight, which boosts Radio One's signal throughout the South of England.

The music played includes several records which have been banned by the BBC. No one ever claims responsibility for the hijack.

APR 30 Three men found guilty in Liverpool Magistrates Court of activities connected with **RADIO CAROLINE**: involved is a mobile disco called the Radio Caroline Roadshow, one is charged with running the disco, one with booking it to play at his hotel, and one with advertising it with a window sticker.

1977

AUG 15 Another successful hijack of a BBC transmitter occurs today. For three hours the broadcast is heard in an area from Cornwall to Hastings.

NOV 15 During an industrial dispute, some striking fireman use a short-wave fire-service transmitter to broadcast messages of support and information to 'counteract the distorted reporting of the strike and its rumours'.

DEC 17 A court in Montpellier dismisses a case brought against **RADIO FIL BLEAU**. The station had started from a shop in Montpellier with the specific aim of challenging the present state monopoly.

The judge declares that the monopoly constitutes a breach of the constitutional right to liberty of expression. An appeal has been lodged by the state prosecution with the High Court in Paris.

1978

FEB 3 The previous two weeks see an onslaught by police against pirate stations in Dublin. There are two main stations: **RADIO DUBLIN** (The Big D) and **ALTERNATIVE RADIO DUBLIN** (ARD). Equipment has been seized but it does not keep the stations off the air longer than a few hours. **Mr John Kelly** former Attorney General questions the constitutional validity of **RTE's** (the national system) monopoly. Loopholes in the Irish laws against broadcasting are exploited more since a court decision that since seized equipment could be used for amplification as well as transmitting there is reasonable doubt whether it is illegal.

APR 26 At Southend Crown Court Judge **Martin Ward** dismisses the case against **RADIO CAROLINE** DJ **Johnny Jason** (real name Rudiger Von Etzdorf). Judge Ward says he is uneasy about asking the jury to decide the issue of whether he had taken part in an unlawful broadcast from the police evidence before them.

However he refuses to award costs to **Johnny Jason** with the comment: 'Here is a young man who, with others, decided to cock a snook at society. When he set foot on that boat and went into the studio he knew he was doing something he should not be doing'.

JUN 7 The French National Assembly passes a law to protect the state of broadcasting monopoly. The punishments are severe: F10,000 to F100,000, and/or a prison sentence of up to a year.

RADIO NOVA IRELAND'S NO. 1 STATION IN ONLY 12 MONTHS OF LIFE

1980

MAR 20 The **Mi Amigo** sinks in rough seas and after being holed on a sandbank. Sinking due to loss of an anchor the day before and drifting from her fixed position. The crew are taken off by the Sheerness lifeboat **Helen Turnbull** in a force ten storm. The **Mi Amigo's** mast remains visible above the surface at 51°31′ North, 1°17′ East near the N.W. Long Sand Beacon.

MAY 22 Thanet Council announces plans to re-float the **Mi Amigo**, and make it into a tourist attraction at a permanent site at Ramsgate, Kent.

OCT 11 HORIZON RADIO begins broadcasting. It is a 2 hour tape on Sunday night, on 102.5FM (stereo). It is London's first Black Music station.

1982

RADIO JACKIE FUND RAISING PROMOTIONS MAKE THEM A POPULAR PIRATE ORGANISATION

JAN 4 A concentrated campaign begins at the Home Office against the pirate stations in London. It is estimated that at present there are about 20 illegal stations in operation throughout the capital. Most stations operate unmanned. They put out low-power transmissions on a subsidiary rig, at around 88 on the FM band, which is picked up, magnified, and broadcast by the main transmitter. The main transmitter has already been set up prior to the broadcast, usually on the top of a tower-block nearby, in the case of FM stations.

Of the stations at present in operation, the following are the most popular:

RADIO JACKIE: on 227 meters, broadcasting from 8am - 6pm on Sundays. It plays adult-oriented rock.

DREAD BROADCASTING CORPORATION (DBC): on 103 mHz FM. Plays reggae, mixed with radical rants every Friday night.

RADIO JFM: on 94 mHz FM, plays jazz-funk and soul throughout London.

HORIZON RADIO: 94.6 mHz FM based in South West London, it plays a similar mix of jazz-funk and soul as **JFM**.

RADIO INVICTA: on 92.4 mHz FM, an all-out soul station, mixed with ads for local discos and record shops, from 10am — midnight throughout London.

RADIO FREE LONDON (RFL): on 92 mHz plays rock, and news throughout London from 2pm to 4am.

103

STUART HENRY

Stuart Henry, the radio pirate who tried every known cure for seasickness to no avail, recorded most of his shows for *Radio Scotland* from land. That same audience keenly followed him to *Radio 1* where his immensely popular show, incorporating a slot for runaway children, made him a household name. Those same householders recoiled in horror as Stuart was fired from the BBC amidst rumours of drug addiction and drink problems. Tragically the truth was worse. Unbeknown to everyone, including the DJ himself, Stuart had developed Multiple Sclerosis — the cause of his stumbling and unco-ordination. Since that discovery, Stuart and his stunning ex-model wife, Ollie, have given moral support to thousands of other sufferers and been unstinting in their efforts to raise money for MS research. Their programme is still beamed out from the Grand Duchy, a high spot on *Radio Luxembourg*.

242

RADIO SCOTLAND'S SHOWBEAT MONTHLY

JUNE, 1966 — Vol. 1. No. 3

ONE SHILLING

RADIO SCOTLAND FIRST PIX

CHRIS McCLURE SECTION — CHEVLONS — SPENCER DAVIS GROUP
EDINBURGH'S BEACHCOMBERS — PAUL YOUNG — FREE CONTESTS

STYLE SPECIAL!

KENNY EVERETT

RADIO LONDON
RADIO ONE
CAPITAL RADIO

Maurice James Christopher Cole, later to be the one and only Kenny Everett, is probably the leading example of how a pirate DJ from the North Sea used the broadcast media to become a nationwide celebrity. From radio to television, Kenny Everett's own brand of wacky humour has earned him the wrath of the programme controllers everywhere and the adoration of legions of fans. In addition, he had the enviable task of being the official pirate radio reporter on The Beatles USA tour, keeping *Radio London* listeners clued up on the every move of the Fab Four.

Kenny Everett, like so many of the English pirate broadcasters, entered the business by a mixture of luck and originality. He must take credit, though, for being the only pirate DJ to be recommended for the job by the BBC...

"I had always been a tape machine fan, for some odd reason, inmy youth, before even video tape had been invented almost. They were still messing around with black and white video in America, for some reason I can't figure out, I used to cut out pictures of these old machines and stick them in books. I was fanatical about video tape and this was before anyone had ever even heard the word video.

That strange obsession came in handy later on because by the the time the video came around I knew everything there was to know about it and we jumped straight into the video show. I was into doing audio tape. I had two tape machines, I used to do little silly shows for friends and by the time '62 came around I was extremely well into messing around with tapes and generally being comfortable with a microphone. So I sent one of these tapes to the BBC eventually, on the advice of a chum who said 'why don't you get paid for doing this instead of just doing it for fun'. I thought it couldn't happen in a million years, because **David Jacobs** and **Pete Murray** are around and who wants another DJ. The tape was called the *Maurice Cole Quarter of an Hour Show* which lasted 20 minutes and they sent me a telegram back about four weeks later, when I had forgotten all about it, saying 'brilliant tape, we are going to broadcast it, come down and be interviewed on the Home Service'. It was a midweek programme called Mid Week, a magazine show.

They broadcast the tape and they interviewed me on the wireless and I said 'have you got any jobs because I like this, this is all fully carpeted and people call you darling'. And they said they 'hadn't got any openings at the moment because this is the BBC but have you heard of this pirate radio thing, ships are flying in from America all over the place, maybe they have got a vacancy'. So on the advice of an individual in the BBC I applied to *Radio London,* sent them the same tape and I was on board the next day honking into the North Sea. Nobody else could do it that way, it was just a lucky series of events, they had just arrived and were desparate for DJs, we need 12 people, anybody want to come and try . . . "

Despite Everett's throwaway attitude to the beginnings of his career, it was his very special talent that enabled him to survive the pressures of the job, noted at this point for the rapid turnover of presenters. Even from the start he is remembered for not towing the partyline . . .
"Some of the terrible people who joined then are still going now.

It was so new and trendy and fab. It was nice to be in on something so fun, it was unusual in a way because I was suddenly scooped up from Liverpool after working in an office and a bakery and all that dull stuff to suddenly be rolling around on the North Sea playing records. Very odd, like being on another planet, it was fun but you couldn't walk in one direction for about a minute without falling off the side, there were no restaurants, you couldn't go for a ride on your bike. It was very restricting, but the pioneering spirit was there, that was fun.

Being the best equipped meant slightly better than nothing at all in those days, because it was all held together with elastic, like we only had one tape machine for six or eight months, so we couldn't do any copying. We had to go from tape machine to cartridge machine and back if we wanted to do any double voices.

The engine room was right next to the studio and there was a thin wall between us so every time they turned the engine on you had to talk closer to the microphone so you couldn't hear this rumbling noise. In fact on all the tapes of *Radio London* that I have heard you could always hear the dynamo going in the background."

There was a feeling of cameraderie in the very beginning, soon overtaken by the basic requirements of competitive business. Kenny Everett witnessed this fairly rapid change of attitude within the pirate business.
"It depends how you looked at it, we all thought we were all fighting against the naughty old boring Beeb, so we were together in that way. But after the figures took off and we had as many or more listeners in the South than the BBC had, then we started having goes at each other.

We had more listeners than *Caroline* did, we had more power than they did, but everybody remembers them more because of the silly name.

I was a virgin in those days, I thought everything was on the surface, and there were no dirty dealings at all. I was very surprised when somebody got shot, I thought how could anybody get shot, we are just sitting around playing records, I didn't know about the politics.

I don't know about politics, I don't care either, I just play records.

I knew it would go on land because there was such a demand for it, so I just thought it was a question of hanging around until it happened — and it won't be long now because people are beginning to wave placards at Parliament. The need had been shown and it was just a question of time, and I went round Broadcasting House trying to get known. I left about six months before they finished, thinking: 'clever move I'll go while they are finishing off at sea and by the time they come I'll be well known at the BBC'. I used to use all sorts of tricks to get into the canteen on the 6th floor and have my name paged, 'could you page Kenny Everett please' and this big booming voice would come over the canteen about once an hour 'paging Mr Kenny Everett', and in about a month I would walk into **Derek Chinnery's** office and say 'hello, I'm looking for a job, I'm a DJ and my name is Kenny Everett'. He would go 'oh, so you're Kenny Everett', he had heard my name over about 17 lunches. I used to wander round Broadcasting House getting used to the layout of the place, always carrying a metal spool in my hand, so they would think I was one of their crowd."

For a very brief moment Kenny joined Dave Cash at *Radio Monte Carlo* and then his career developed to encompass television, a stage which made him a household name.
"It was the tiniest interlude in my life, they said 'we've got this megawatt station in the South of France would you do some programmes for us', so I went into the studio and did one show for them and then I was told they were packing up their British interests.

Cash was involved a lot, for ages before I came along, by the time he persuaded me it was a good idea they had closed up.

KENNY EVERETT IN THE GUISE OF 'CUDDLY KEN', FROM HIS LIGHTHEARTED
AUTOBIOGRAPHY, PUBLISHED BY WILLOW BOOKS

It seems to follow on that if you do radio you can do television as well, in this case it happened to be just about correct, the two things are wildly different of course...

The telly bit gets you well known suddenly and quickly but as they will all tell you, radio is more fun, it is like a hobby really. You go on and it is all your own work and you are responsible to yourself for what goes out.

Whereas in television it is a group effort from the hundreds of different people and if it comes together you can't say 'hey, I did that' because it is the work of a hundred people.

On radio you get free LPs, that's nice, and you get quite a fair cheque at the end of it and you get a nice feeling if you've done a good show, but you can't plan that

KENNY EVERETT AS MAURICE COLE

though. Many is the time I've gone in stacked up to the teeth with tapes and stuff and you sit down and it just goes and you do a terrible show, it is in the lap of gods. Sometimes you go in and you're hung over and you feel like nothing, and something goes ** and the show is terrific. The best bit is you get a nice feeling if it has been a good show.

Recently I did a really naff show, I just couldn't get myself off the ground and I left the studio nearly in tears and last week I did quite a good one, strange that, it doesn't get any easier or any more difficult. In the old days I used to think I should plan more, but you can't, it *is* in the lap of the gods.''

The appearance of a new wave of pirates is a matter of no concern to Kenny, although he still rates *Radio London* **as one of life's milestones . . .**
"I don't think its important at all, it just means we have got a better choice on thedial now instead of one station doing 200 different things, you've got 200 stations all doing one thing quite well.

Radio London was totally important. I would probably be back in Liverpool now if it hadn't been for the pirates, because you couldn't get into the BBC, it was a closed shop.''

The guy who recommended me to join the pirates has since been fired. You can't kick the system, the best thing is to leave it and come back and if you are already famous they say 'oh come in'.''

The move to television, and the tremendous success it brought, was a major development in Kenny Everett's career. One which his inventive mind capitalised on, although his irreverence for the television system, as with his own brand of radio material, kept him poised on the edge of impending disasters . . .

"I think that is why we got famous on Thames Television because we did scratch our nose and we did things that were considered not done on TV — like Hot Gossip; you just don't do that sort of thing on TV, wriggle your arse and things. What we did is we just relaxed in front of the camera, like I had been doing on the radio for all those years, but it was right for then and people are doing it all over the place now, they are scratching their arses too. **Jules Holland** is it?

They have gone too far, the next thing they'll be farting and fucking on TV, that will be the next step. I shan't be watching of course.''

The days on *Radio London* **were quite controlled in their own way, although Everett is remembered as the jock who would never stick to the schedules, often pushing it to the point of being taken off air . . .**
"We didn't have absolute freedom, they just hadn't invented any laws and they expected us to be very irresponsible, some of us were.

It was fairly rigid, **Tony Windsor** would tell you about that, he was the guy who brought it over from Australia, the fact that you just didn't go on and play what you liked. It seemed a good idea, he drew out a list of things 1-10, 10-30, oldie, climber, etc., in rotation. It is a good idea really because you have to play lots of famous stuff and oldies that you might have missed otherwise, we stuck to that because if we didn't he would run down into the studio and rap our knuckles.''

Kenny Everett's career has left the *Galaxy* **a long way behind, and although there is no nostalgia for the old days he acknowledges a permanent link with the old team . . .**
" . . . it's like relatives, you are born with a set of relatives and you can't get away from them and you are expected to go to their weddings and funerals and parties and things — and you sit there stullified, it is like that. It's a family, but they are not people you would seek out at a party and sit beside. There were a lot of nice people — but there were also obviously people that you wouldn't spend a lot of time with . . . you were just stuck with them.

When I see **Dave Cash** we always have a natter and a cup of tea, and a couple of others. **Tommy Vance** is a great mate as well, it is nice to see some of them. Funny way to start out though, being stuck together with 40 strange people on a boat.

I was sick on the tender going out to the boat, the first day, honking over the side, and as night fell and I was looking at the lights and swaying about because it was in the middle of a storm and I thought: 'I'd give my legs to be on that shore line now'. But the Tender Company had a strike, as soon as they dropped us they went off for three months so I had to get used to it. But it was fairly hairy.

As for quitting and going back to Liverpool; Good Heavens no, I would rather be sick.''

109

JOHN PEEL

**VARIOUS (USA)
RADIO LONDON
RADIO ONE**

John Peel, voted Britain's top disc jockey 11 times in a row by the Melody Maker, is almost a pirate DJ by accident. His actual time aboard the *Galaxy* as a *Radio London* DJ was minimal and yet it is his method of broadcasting that makes him readily identifiable with the spirit of pirate radio. He is an unlikely candidate for such affiliations. An ex-public school boy and National Seviceman, under his real name of John Ravenscroft, who got into radio in America in 1961 by way of his rare collection of blues records and his ability to read their French labels. The Beatle boom and the corresponding interest in Liverpudlians gave Peel a leg up in the radio business and he ended up as a top jock in California. It was to be a dif-

ferent world in English broadcasting.

Peel returned from his successful period in California to the UK as one of those rarities amongst the English radio contingent, an experienced commercial broadcaster.
"I had been working on radio in America since 1961, initially Dallas, Texas; then I got into it full time as a Beatle expert in Oklahoma City in '64/65. I was in California for a year and a half in San Bernadino, came back here in '67 and was by and large unemployable at the time.

I hadn't anything to come home to. Just luck really, being in the right place at the right time, music lovers might argue the wrong place at the wrong time. Where my mother lives in Notting Hill, the bloke living in the next house was something in advertising and did a lot of business with *Radio London* and knew **Alan Keene** who was in charge of it all. He said 'why didn't I go down and talk to Alan Keene'. So I did and they must have known then that they were going to be closed down shortly and, because I had been working on the radio in California, they didn't even make me do an audition — which is probably just as well under the circumstances. I went on there and did a regular Top 40 programme.

Because the last man on had to double up, junior of the team, I started doing the midnight to two spot, then it dawned on me over a period of time that the lads upstairs were playing cards, or gone to bed, or watching blue films or something. I gradually dispensed with the format and it wasn't until **Brian Epstein** phoned Alan Keene and congratulated him on having the foresight to put on this excellent programme late at night and they all thought 'we'd better listen to this'; when they heard it they were all slightly horrified but it had gone too far for them to stop it really . . .''

Peel went aboard the *Galaxy* when the cult of the pirate radio was at it's height. In typical Peel fashion this aspect of the job escaped him to begin with . . .
"I wasn't aware, I had been home only a couple of times since 1960 and I knew the pirates existed and so on but I had no idea of how important they were or the impact that they had on people or the impact they had on popular music at the time.

It was tame by comparison with California, there were a lot of things you would have been fired for, the stations working out there were about as hard as Top 40 radio has ever got, it had a very heavy commercial edge. You were only allowed to talk over fade or introductions to records, no talking over the air and you had to operate a jingle which identified the station and you were allowed to forget it once and the second time you forgot it you became like an un-person and no reference would ever be made to you again. You just disappeared off the earth and obviously *Radio London* was nothing like that at all.

At the time I was coming to the end of a fairly catastrophic marriage and I was pleased to be on the ship because my wife was amazingly aggressive and she hit me a lot and so I was pleased to be on the ship for two weeks out of three.

It wasn't that bad. I found there were appalling rough days and a lot of quite nice aspects, myself and a couple of engineers used to go up to the, I'm sure it is called something like the storm deck, but the highest bit of the ship anyway, and close down the hatch and smoke your illegal substances up there. By and large fairly wasted. This was just passing the time, and because I was a very reflective youth and spent most of my life trying to have beautiful thoughts, I used to spend a lot of time sitting on some of the car tyres, hanging over the edge looking at the sea and thinking deep thoughts about sea gulls.

There was a play list and commercials that had to be done and various station things that had to be gone through, but as I say after midnight I virtually did away with them, to the point where I didn't bother to do the news or the weather or anything. Just to do two hours of records and reading other peoples poetry very badly.

I saw **Johnnie Walker** from time to time, who I liked very much and have always regarded Johnnie Walker as being one of the disc jockeys' disc jockey; and when people I know talk about radio the subject of Johnnie Walker always comes up and I don't know whether it is because of his own integrity really. But I think he is the best broadcaster *Radio 1* ever had anyway.''

The Marine Offences Act appeared very quickly on Peel's horizon as he gazed out to sea, but it was one of those clouds with a silver lining as it led, surprisingly, to a post with *Radio 1*.
"I enjoyed what I was doing as I enjoy it now and didn't really care very much for the idea of it being cut short soon after I joined. But I didn't think I had much of a chance of being taken on by *Radio 1* and ironically in the photograph of all the *Radio 1* people, taken on the church steps, a classic photograph, I am the only survivor now that **Blackburn** has moved off.

If you had looked at that photograph at the time you would think 'they'll get rid of that bugger'.

I've always admired the BBC, because I came to it all so late, I didn't have these romantic pirate notions that other people had. So much came along afterwards like these things always do, at the time it was just like a job for people who were by and large unemployable and it didn't seem particularly romantic at the time.

It was something that I liked doing, because I like doing radio programmes. I would do them for anybody really, I don't want to get into television or play Hamlet or anything like that, I just want to play radio.''

John Peel was part of that magic moment at Liverpool Street when the DJ's arrived to a chaotic welcome after the radio stations had closed down. It was a scene reminiscent of Beatle mania . . .
"I went when everybody else did. We took the train to Liverpool Street, all the stars were there and I was wearing my kaftan and bells and beads and looked grotesque. We all got off the train and there were several thousand people there and I walked through the crowd and nobody recognised me, so I walked round the back of the station and went through again and they still didn't recognise me despite my natural modesty and boyish charm.

I went straight onto *Radio 1*, I was one of the first lot on *Radio 1* and I think it was mainly because, obviously, *Radio 1* had no real idea what they were doing so they had to take people off the pirate ships because there wasn't anybody else. It wasn't as though there were dozens of people who were qualified DJs, we were on very short

THE FAMOUS STAMPEDE AT LIVERPOOL STREET STATION

term contracts initially.

Funnily enough, there were more disciplines on *London,* they banned more records. *Radio 1* always gets slagged off for banning records, they don't ban that many, the pirate ships used to ban a lot more and for the most peculiar reasons. You always assume at some stage you are going to go through periods when you are restricted by the requirments of the people that you work for, but you just get in there and try and work it all until you have got what you want. I did that on the pirate ships, just taking advantage of the fact that nobody was listening and the same sort of thing here now..."

Peel is forever fixed in the public's mind as a pirate radio DJ even though his time onboard ship was brief and towards the end of the period. It is as much to do with his continuing attitude towards broadcasting music as anything else . . .
"I was on ship from February or March — so about 6 months in all. At the time the kind of programme I was doing, obviously nobody else was doing anything like it, just as well you might argue, but it was very popular, the last couple of weeks I was getting 10 times as much mail as everybody else put together, it was an extraordinary situation.

I don't really believe the *Radio 1* show was a cult myself, I think it is the kind of ground roots of everything else that goes on. The trouble is it is romantic to put yourself in a ghetto and present yourself as the Bader Meinhof gang of broadcasting, but it is just another aspect of what *Radio 1* does.

It seems to me my post here is . . . all these other blokes are doing this and playing these records and here am I playing things you're not going to get to hear otherwise. I don't see it as a revolutionary breakthrough."

The group of presenters who originate from the pirate boats remain colleagues of Peel's but he doesn't admit to any special affinity with them because of the past; the days on the pirate ship are clearly but a small part of his broadcasters life . . .
"I might do if I ever saw any of the other people who I was working with, but **Blackburn** I see from time to time, and I quite like. I used to hate him, I thought he was like the anti-Christ, but I quite like him, because we have quite a bit in common.

The other people, **Chuck Blair**, and **Lorne King** where are they now?

Johnnie Walker is the only one I would like to see really, because well-off **Kenny Everett** with his remarks on **Michael Foot** has just become a sexist dickhead.

Viewed globally, cosmically, it was all totally unimportant really; but from the point of view of the development of popular music in this country and obviously popular radio it was quite clearly critical, it is the kind of king pin of the whole thing.

If it hadn't happend, I suspect that radio in this country would be like popular radio is in most other European countries. This is one of the things these people who criticise *Radio 1* and I criticise it myself, but what we all forget is if you go and live somewhere like Sweden you get about three hours of popular music a day and the rest is whatever it is they do in Sweden . . ."

The new landbased pirates are of interest to John Peel, in a way they both work in a similar vein,
but any nostalgic return to the early pirate radio idioms gets little response from him.
"I think they are quite good, I listen to *Horizon* quite a lot and *DBC* and I quite like the idea just because I like listening to them. I think there should be a wider range of choices. I think there is a danger with a monopoly like *Radio 1* that they become smug and self satisfied and there are things I think *Radio 1* could learn from pirate stations, although the consideration is for the music and not for the egos of the DJs.

I wish they would pay attention to the pirate stations, what they are doing is whacking out the music not bereft of personality — but there is not the obsession with self which, no names, but there are nationally known DJs whose admiration for themselves knows no bounds.

There are a lot of people who regard the '60s . . . I think the '60s are a pain in the arse, because of the preoccupation of producers and DJs with the '60s who feel this was a time when they were young. If they can keep the '60s going they can keep themselves young as well, I do think that is the reason for doing it.

This seems to me to be a complete nonsense. I'm the oldest of the lot except for **Savile** and *I* don't want to do it. Although some of the others were the same age as me once, they seemed to have dropped a couple of years recently . . ."

Peel is not the only professional radio man to be quizzical about the successful new ship *Radio Laser*, and he is not alone in wondering where the funding is coming from:
"I do listen to *Laser*, it worries me a little bit because they seem to be increasingly hitting on news coverage, the kind of hard American white politics. You start to wonder how the whole thing is funded; because a ship arrives with a full complement of operators and library in the middle of the sea and starts broadcasting away with no visible means of support. You start to think young people in northern Europe are seen as a disruptive element as far as American policies go because they don't agree with them.

The original *Radio London* was funded by oil people from mid-Texas. Obviously she (**Ladybird Johnson**) didn't come over and tell us what to say politically, I don't understand how *Laser* is funded and I would like to know . . .

I like what they are doing because they tend to get on with it. I don't approve of segue-ing vast numbers of records, I don't listen to it that often that I know. When I am in the car I listen to the BBC World Service which I still think is the best thing BBC does.

They will find some way of controlling and restricting community radio if they do legalise it, it would be in an emasculated form. Unlike America, where the money is there to finance an enormous number of commercial radio stations, there isn't enough money in various communities here to pay their way so there won't be enough to finance a whole stack of stations."

1983

JAN 5 According to a Gallop poll nearly four million listeners tune into **RADIO CAROLINE** every day.

FEB 28 **RADIO HORIZON** becomes a 24 hour station. Since its foundation it has had 27 transmitters seized. Its audience has now grown to a million, according to a spokesman.

MAR The **Ross Revenge** originally the **Freyr** built in West Germany in 1960 is harboured in Santander, Spain, undergoing conversion to a radio ship. Reportedly owned by the Grotham Steamship Lines Inc.

MAY 24 A statement from the Dept of Trade and Industry claims that high priority is being given dealing with illegal broadcast 'with the resources available'. Letters are being sent out to advertisers using land-based pirates warning them of the consequences. However, the Chairman of the IBA **Lord Thompson** declares that he is 'disappointed by the level of effective action', and condemns the 'apparent condoning of theft and other instances of lawbreaking accompanied by a worrying unwillingness to deal with the matter'.
The D.T.I. states that it has had 21 successful prosecutions for illegal broadcasting in the last year.

Seventeen miles off Clacton,

NEW SHIP — OLD GIRL, THE ROSS REVENGE

RIGHT: BEHIND THE MIKE OF *RADIO LASER*

from the MV **Communicator**, a former Lowestoft coaster, **RADIO LASER** begins broadcasting. The ship has been re-equipped in Florida by **LASER'S** parent company International through a company registered in Panama, Eurad SA.
It plays 20 hours a day non-stop 'all-hit music' as its call-sign says, on 558 meters with 25kw power. After its initial broadcasts it runs into opposition from the Irish community in Britain because the strong signal is interfering with **RADIO TELEFIS EIREANN**, the Irish radio service.

AUG 5 The Telecommunications Act comes into torce. Its main provisions are: the DTI's Radio Interference Service becomes the Radio Investigation Service, with increased powers, ie they may now seize pirate or other

love from caroline

illegal broadcasting equipment pending prosecution. The police can arrest without a warrant if they believe a suspect has given a false name and address.
Pirates now face a maximum of £2,000 fine, and/or three months in gaol. **Steve Fox**, of **RADIO SKYLINE**, says 'it won't make a bit of difference to **RADIO SKYLINE**. The laws of the land are made. Whether they are implemented remains to be seen'.
AUG 9 **RADIO CAROLINE** returns to the air on 963 kHz

(319 meters), broadcasting from the MV **Ross Revenge**. The first record played is 'Caroline' by the Fortunes. Renamed **IMAGINE** Registered in Panama, has offices in Los Angeles, and is supplied from Spain.
At a party to re-launch the station in the Lyceum Ballroom, **RADIO ONE** DJ **Tony Blackburn** pulls his trousers down and moons in protest at the poor response from other DJs, he says: 'I was disappointed because DJ's who have made it today made it thanks to **RADIO CAROLINE**

didn't show up. I encouraged the audience to get off their backsides and do something'.

SEPT 19 **SKYLINE RADIO** comes on air based near Elephant and Castle, its target is South-East London. Its daytime format is Top-40, with specialist music (such as high-energy disco) at the weekends. It broadcasts on 1413 kHz (212 meters) and 90.2 FM (mono).

DEC 8 **RADIO SUNSHINE** a local radio covering an area round Ludlow in Shropshire is closed by magistrates.
Graham Symonds, an unemployed electrician, built and ran the station from Villa Farm, Greet, near Ludlow. It was staffed by volunteers, and organised many local charity ventures including a cricket match between **RADIO SUNSHINE** and the local police station!

1984

Twenty years after *Radio Caroline* came on air, the station, along the the other North Sea pirates, *Radio Laser 558*, is again front page news. Whilst the 'old lady' continues to broadcast 'Loving Awareness' and music, Ronan's own brand of pop philosophy, *Laser* is scooping up the audience ratings. The effect of this American manned station, based aboard the M.V. Communicator, has had serious repercussions for IBA stations in London and the East Coast. At *Capital Radio*, audience losses have resulted in a shake up of policy and staff, with some well known faces getting the 'cheerio'. At Essex ILR stations audience ratings have plummeted.

The so-called mystery surrounding *Laser* is based on the fact that it carries (as yet) no advertising. Speculation regarding the funding for the U.S. based company, American crew and broadcast staff goes from the sublime to the ridiculous, with the C.I.A. being cited as one source of money. The London Evening Standard in a series of articles about the station claimed to have discovered that BBC newsman, Roger Parry, acts as 'adviser and co-ordinator', and that the owner is Irish multi-millionaire, Philip Smythe.

Parry has denied these reports as 'bizarre' and 'nonsense' and, naturally, Philip Smythe was not available for comment. The source for these leads came from members of the *Laser 558* set-up team who had then parted with the company; they were also the source for the launch costs estimate of $2,000,000.

There has been a continual fear in Government circles that the power, quality and sophistication of *Laser* might be used for political broadcasting, however subtle, a factor always denied by the station spokesman, Roy Lindau. From New York Lindau replied to enquiry's regarding the funding of *Laser* by stating the station may close if advertising pencilled in for October (1984) wasn't realised. Previously no mention of the station closing had been made.

Roger Parry's position, (if as described by the Standard and supported by Bernard Gelman of the Florida based transmitter installation company, and ex-DJ Paul Rusling, an engineer and Standard informant), is a delicate one. The clear breach of the Marine Offences Act, would open

THE M.V. COMMUNICATOR RIDING THE WAVES OF CONTROVERSY

Parry up to prosecution if the allegations prove true, whilst Philip Smythe as an Irish citizen would be immune. Parry's association with the BBC would prove a tremendous embarrassement to the authorities, who are bringing big guns to bear in the case after reports that the M.V. Communicator is tendered from Essex and that it's personnel are ashore doing promotions.

Meanwhile, reports that conditions on board the Ross Revenge are deteriorating continue and rumours that the *Caroline* jocks have to use the *Laser* ship to get a shower as they have no hot water are gaining credence.

Whilst DJ and promoter Tony Prince was visiting the *Laser* offices in New York, a telex stating that Atlantic City money was going to launch *Wonderful Radio London* on the anniversary of the demise of the sixties station based aboard the Galaxy, caused quite a stir. The 14th of August (3.00pm) came and went with no new addition to the North Sea.

The landbased pirates on the mainland regard the mounting D.T.I. and police activity, instigated by *Laser*, and to a much lesser extent by *Caroline*, with increasing horror. At South London pirate *Jackie* there is a growing conviction that a local broadcast licence is only months away and *Laser* is making waves in more ways than one. An unspoken 'arrangement' between the Post Office and the reactionary London pirates may dissolve into a broadcasting backlash, whilst the radical stations are expecting one anyway.

It is a different story in Ireland, the country that seems to be, if Mr Smythe does own *Laser*, the pirates 'tropical isle'. It is the home of the boss pirate station *Nova* and birthplace, not to be forgotten, of Ronan O'Rahilly. In Dublin *Nova* is run by Chris Carey, once known as Spangles Muldoon of *Radio Caroline* and *RNI* fame. Primarily a radio engineer Carey has taken *Nova* to the top of the Irish radio charts with a quality sound, superb facilities and a signal that hits the West Midlands loud and clear.

Based in Nova Park, just outside Dublin, the station boasts its own disco on site that works hand in hand with the radio. Nova Park itself is a local tourist attraction with a constant flow of visitors and sightseers. The enthusiasm and expertise of Carey, one of the most experienced of broadcasters, is the source of *Nova's* success. Everything is produced to the highest quality — a major plus to advertisers — and the equipment would match any IBA company, and be the source of envy and amazement to most UK pirate studios. Most of the sound is produced on the self cueing cartridge system at *Nova*, an American style that is still slow to catch on in Britain, very few discs are actually played on air. After early brushes with the law, *Nova* is left to it's own devices, wisely steering well clear of politics in a troubled Ireland; a recent poll gave the station 60%+ of the Irish audience and the advertising income matches this programming success.

The feeling is optimistic. Public opinion is for localised radio and organisations like *Jackie* have proved it can work. Whether a system of licencing will be introduced remains to be seen, what is certain is that any British Government is loathe to release a free form of communication into the hands of the public; the comment by the Home Office's Lord Wells-Pestell is well worth noting: "I think we have to seriously consider the enormous disadvantages of having a vast army of people who can communicate with one another very easily..."

TOP: HOLLY MICHAELS AT *LASER* ABOVE: THE *CAROLINE* JOCKS THANKING GOD FOR THE JOB

RADIO JACKIE

Peter Rivers acts as the public relations man for *Radio Jackie*, **the most successful landbased pirate station in the UK. Successful because it has managed to flourish in a semi-official manner whilst still being outside the law. The long history of the South London station gives it a credibility lacking in more recent launches . . .**

"The station first went on air back in March 1969, so it has been going for well over 15 years. The original reason why it went on air was there existed a group of people who thought that after the demise of the '60s pirates and off-shore stations, a lot of the benefit that they had brought had been lost and nothing had really taken its place. OK you had *Radio 1,* the one national station, but no commercial radio at that time and the group that was formed was a group of radio enthusiasts about 18 or 19 years old called Sutton Commercial Radio Association. Basically their aim was to campaign for something similar to *Caroline* or *London* being on-shore but on a much more limited basis, a sort of commercial radio station playing music for a small area, that is why it is called Sutton Commercial Radio Association.

One of the original founder members is still involved with the station, **Mike Knight**, and certain other members. They campaigned and wrote letters that the Government should be doing more and that it wasn't good enough just to close down the options and they thought that perhaps one of the best ways of really making their point was to go on air themselves, which they did in March 1969.

Programming at *Jackie* **has matured as the station has consolidated it's position but to achieve a fixed studio base didn't happen over night.**

"It was basically pop music because both the people running the station then were 18 or 19 year olds, it was music that was either being played on *Radio 1* or not being heard at all. They tried to put in some local information about the area, which is why they were different to other stations. That continued through to the '70s, as you get into the early '70s that extended on a Sunday and started creeping up to three or four hours and then a whole afternoon's programme. You are still basically talking about field operations, the transmitter taken out each Sunday morning and someone would go and actually have to set up the whole transmitter site, sometimes the same place would be used several weeks running depending if they had been visited or not. Every so often transmissions would be cut short because there was a visit by members of the Post Office tracking teams.

The fact that you were only on for three hours, by the time they had tracked you down and found you, you had probably finished your transmissions anyway, but even so you are talking about being raided once every five or six weeks on average. It seemed to vary, some year you would get a lot of action then it would go quite for a year or two."

The re-emergence of the pirate ships had a negative effect on the *Jackie* **staff but the station was undergoing a steady evolution and developing a local identity. It helped encourage some of those involved to keep going . . .**

"I think there were several times when people thought they might as well give it all up, and particularly so after 1970 when you had off-shore pirates coming back again. First you had *RNI* in the early '70s, the return of *Caroline*

PETER RIVERS AT *JACKIE* HQ

and so on in 72/73. All the time you had the Dutch ones.

You get a bit put off after being continually busted and programmes ending half way through and people recording programmes which were never actually transmitted because the station didn't go on air. There were a lot of technical problems as well, actually setting up everything from scratch, somedays the chances were that the wind would be too strong and the aerial wouldn't go up or something would go wrong, or tapes would arrive at the wrong speed, a lot of things to put people off.

I think the biggest thing that also put people off is in 1973 when they actually started legal commercial radio, some of the ideas originally behind *Jackie* then seemed to be put into effect. In fact they even used a tape of *Radio Jackie* in the House of Commons Committee where they were discussing the same Broadcasting Bill to the one which was eventually passed in 1972, and introduced ILR controlled by the IBA in 1973.

One of the MPs, **Austin Mitchell** actually put on a tape of *Radio Jackie* to demonstrate to some of the MPs what commercial radio could sound like if it was allowed.

This was quite a momentous event, in fact it was the first tape that had ever been played in the House of Commons — they had to have a big legal debate as to whether they could even play the tape; and eventually some indication was given of how they rated it and how well it could sound.

The management of the company changed with the pressures of commercial business, and with the right structure the South London station made admirable progress:

"Throughout that time and right up until the middle of 1983 it was run by a Committee, which sounds very nice and democratic, it had eight people and occasionally you let people in and had big public meetings with all the staff and 40 odd people cramped into a hall and trying to make sense. That was fine, it was as good as a Committee ever is, it was o.k. to produce a programme for eight or nine hours on a Sunday and people had other jobs throughout the week and would get together and make sure it was going to happen.

December 1982 was when *Jackie* decided to go 24 hours to test the water and see what would happen as the first London British land based station to do so. It soon became obvious in the early stages of '83, in fact we had successfully gone on for quite a few months despite a couple of raids, really the Committee is very unwieldy. Say if the GPO were to suddenly arrive you can't convene a meeting of eight people to decide who should be spokesman or whatever, whereas in the past all the guys would actually be around to decide in the middle of the field.

Once you had gone 24 hours it was a static site, someone's house, basically there was no one around apart from the guy who lived there, so it had to be sorted out and also the overheads, costs, expenses, studio equipment,

EX-390 DJ ROB RANDALL IN THE HOT SEAT

everything else was on a such bigger scale than it had been when it was a one day a week operation.

The Committee was arguing and never agreed and eventually **Tony Collis** who was actually a member of the Committee and the Station Engineer offered, because he had the financial resources, to become owner and actually employ people directly and people had certain jobs allocated which would be much more constructive and easy to operate. The Committee agreed that this was a better course of action although it would mean a lot of the members really taking the second row it was better for the station as a whole.

It was agreed that Tony should become the owner and he was prepared to bail the station out as he certainly had to do.

If we were licenced the advertising would be much healthier; with the rates, we wouldn't up them considerably because that would defeat our purpose as a station which small advertisers can afford, but at least it would mean you could be getting more. It was often difficult to do and for several weeks running costs have not been met by the advertising, so he has had to fork out of his own pocket; and there aren't many people around willing to do that consistently.

The current position stems from the latter half of '83 when people were actually allocated various jobs, and *Jackie* now employs a full time staff, up until that time everyone did it as a hobby, it was all part time.

The first full time staff weren't employed until September of '83 when we opened our shop in Morden, and we needed someone to work there and that was *Jackie's* first full time employee; we now have five full time. There is the Advertising Manager who is on commission but working full time, two people in the shop, Head of Presentation, then we have four or five freelancers, who are people like **Rob Randell** who reads the news and does a daily programme and are in effect full timers. The rest of the staff are voluntary."

The GPO tracking systems have the odds in their favour when dealing with land based broadcasters — who are at an obvious disadvantage. The station technicians go to ingenious lengths to avoid meeting the GPO's officials.

"They could track the transmitter site easily enough, in fact they have visited it in the past, but of course they could also track the link transmitter, although you might have some indication if they came and switched the medium wave off, you would know if they switched off the link. Also it is harder for them to track because medium wave is what we publically announce and anyone can tune into it on any radio; whereas the FM links aren't announced and it is harder to find them anyway and they are very directional and low powered and unless they were directly in line they wouldn't be able to pick it up.

The transmitter is not staffed at all, it is in a shed, it is fairly obvious where it is because of the height of the mast and aerial, someone lives in the house and it is part of the grounds, but he is not paid to be there sitting on top of it all the time."

Whilst many ex-pirate jocks have scorned community radio stations as 'scout meetings and jumble sales', *Jackie* has taken an interesting interpretation of the wide 'community' brief . . .

"Initially, *Jackie* was primarily a pop station, it served the local community but it's basis was pop music, that has changed over the last six or eight months.

We have decided that South West London is a relatively affluent part of London and if you look at it democratically there tends to be a high proportion of elderly people. Some stations would have as their main goal to provide a certain type of music service like soul, jazz, funk or whatever, our aim is to serve South West London, so therefore people tune into us because it is local news, local information, local events, advertising etc. They might like some of the music, they might not like some of the music we play but we try to appeal to the broadest possible audience. You have to cater for people over 25 as well as under, and we thought it was easier from the music point of view to cater for 25 plus age group, because a lot of young people can enjoy old music hits from the '60s and '70s and perhaps even the '50s that they have never even heard of before, that music can be very popular with young people whereas I don't think it is the case with old people enjoying music of today. So you spread it out and then pick up a big audience, we are not competing directly with *Radio 1* and it seems not with *Capital Radio* either, but competing much more for the *Radio 2, Radio 4* audience. Which has a lot of benefits for us in that, politically, it is on safer ground.

We want to have councillors and MPs and people like that supporting us to make sure the station can continue and I think it is far easier with the programmes like we have than it would be if we were a 15 to 25 year old range with non stop funk music.

Influential people, people who can vote, people who can write letters to MPs and the papers, and so on, that is the sort of audience we want to aim for and can best serve. We are aiming for a general audience in South West London, it is the prime reason why people tune into us.

Rob Randall has worked for *Radio 390* and I know in the '60s he worked at *BFPS*, he's worked at *Radio Sovereign* before that was closed down last year. People like **Dave Owen** have worked on *Radio Caroline* and stations like *Piccadilly* and *Beacon,* there are other people here who have only worked in what can be called unlicensed stations."

The station's overtures to local Government have paid off, and by presenting a respectable front to the world *Jackie* has survived the legal backlash against the new off-shore pirates. The question hanging over the studios in Morden is: how long? The station is anxious to apply for authorisation as a local broadcast unit . . .

"Sutton Council voted by either 36 or 39 votes, but certainly some margin like that with no votes against and just 10 abstentions, of supporting our application. What we have made is an application booklet to the Home Secretary asking for an experimental licence in South West London.

We are not saying 'we are *Jackie* we've been here 15 years therefore we should have this licence ad infinitum', what we are saying is the Government could use us as an experiment to see if it is viable commercially. They have that in their power to do at any stage and they could also grant it for six months or a year and then review the situation. At the moment there is no application to apply for, there is no licence to apply for, it would be different if there was. They treat London as a whole and there are two stations; a talk station and a music station, *Capital* has just had their's renewed and it not likely to come up for another six or seven years, what we are saying is if someone said 'here's a licence, for a station to broadcast to South West London we could apply for it', not to say we would be the only people, we might lose out, but at least we've brought in community radio at that level which is what we want to do."

RADIO NOVA

Chris Carey, the head of the most successful pirate station ever, *Radio Nova,* **has a dual existance as Spangles Muldoon, the** *Caroline* **DJ and engineer extraordinary. Carey's career in broadcasting covers all aspects of the business, beginning in a humble radio shop in Chester . . .**

"I sent away countless tapes to *Caroline* and got either no reply at all, or standard letters saying, 'thank you for your effort, but we have no vacancies for your style', then they started advertising for engineers. This was obviously a problem I got to know, that they are hard to find, and I rang up and said 'I'm an engineer', forgot all about the disc jockey, let's just sell the engineering bit, and that was it, even though I had only worked on small tiny equipment compared to what they had it was the same basis. That is all they wanted — a technical person to go out.

I went down and met **Chris Moore** then got all tangled up with the disc jockeys, so although I got in the car to go down to Chesterfield Gardens to meet somebody to be an engineer, I got all tangled up with **Andy Archer** and **Stevi Merike** I went in an did an audition and by the grace of God I got it. It was weeks later that they found out that I had also gone for the job of engineer, once on the ship I could do two jobs, so I stayed there.

I had listened to this *Caroline North* ship which was so like Disneyland, to actually go out on the tender which was a filthy, smelly, oil ridden contraption . . . still I thought 'this is o.k., when I get out there I will see this ocean liner, all white, maids flitting around the bedrooms and everything'. When we arrived it was a bit battered, the tenders had banged against it endlessly and knocked all dents in the side, all dirty filthy tyres hanging over which made continuous daily tendering possible without which the ship would have been a wreck.

Nobody was terribly interested in meeting anybody, it was a bit like a public school in that if you weren't known it was like 'what are you doing here'.

For the first two or three weeks, certainly the first two or three days, people like **Johnnie Walker, Robbie Dale** — just ignored you, who were you to encroach on their own little place."

Chris's introduction to Ireland was almost accidental. Again it stemmed through his interests in electronics and propelled him once again into the pirate radio business . . .

"**Brian McKenzie** who was working as a disc jockey on *North Sea* went to Ireland and started a recording studio, to make commercials for pirate stations. I was not interested but helped him.

He saw I was selling this one board computer hand over fist, and one Saturday he said 'you've just taken about three grand in the time I have been talking to you', and I said 'yes, you should be selling this stuff in Ireland, it is really hot'.

So he started taking the stuff to Ireland and opened a company up in Ireland which I never came near.

Then we sold a computer and it went wrong, he sold it to an insurance company and I said 'I'll go over', he had been badgering me to go over anyway to see these pirate stations. Went over fixed the computer in minutes and he took me on a tour of pirate stations.

Then a little bit of magic was kindled again, you see these filthy, filthy studios, with tape recorders like the one you have there to play commercials on, it was all hit and miss what came on, the disc jockeys were terrible, there was not a clue of anything and I kept asking the same question 'do you never get closed down' 'No, never happens year in year out' and I knew what they had got and they didn't.

So I started a station called *Sunshine.* To cut it short I got excited and thought 'damn it, I'll do twelve grand' and these stations were started up for £400, so twelve grand was going to buy the world.

I had a few ideas about how things should be done, a nice hotel which we did in the Sands Hotel, where *Sunshine* is at the moment, and we would have a proper aerial, and a proper broadcasting transmitter, not a home made thing, we brought a second hand thing from BBC and we brought a lot of old broadcasting equipment from stations that were replacing equipment.

We had proper cart machines, proper grams, a bit of a console, proper mixer, proper aerial, the whole thing was you might say proper. It was the nearest thing to like a cheap radio ship but it was no sea.

We put it on and it was successful, I was with it for about two months. I didn't get on personally with a guy called **Robbie Dale**, we just had different ideas, it just didn't gel.

I had been in business on my own several times and knew the ups and downs of playing with cash and Robbie didn't, he wanted to strut about the place and be jack the lad, he hadn't worked out that you don't do that for five years, you put your head down, get the bread, get the security and then you pop up and say 'here I am folks, I've made it'.

We just didn't gel, so I said 'look Robbie I'm out of *Sunshine*', and another director wanted out at the same time.

We both got our money and I went back to America and started a factory in America making Sinclair one board computers, and that was printing money.

We bought a house in California, which we still have and Brian McKenzie kept phoning me up saying 'Robbie Dale is blacking you all over Ireland that you couldn't stay the pace' and it got me really mad and I said 'he can't be saying that, I just left, end of an era, no bad feeling and I am busy doing this'.

So I put the phone down and got a trade paper for radio station equipment and started buying again, new transmitter, this time great stuff, no messing around, knowing that the Government do not take your gear away and you don't get closed down. We put turntables in and ITC cart machines and a brand new FM transmitter because I knew in California FM was so big, and it was opposite here. They didn't have FM in Ireland they had mono and nobody bothered with it, it was so bad, sometimes on, sometimes off.

I brought back a real pukka stereo FM transmitter with all bits you need to make really good studios, hired a flash building in Herbert Street, which was unheard of for a pirate station to move into this sort of area and pay this sort of rent. I must have put in about £100,000 in equipment, front rent and I did another £20,000 on wages, we didn't accept ads, we just came on, the nearest thing to perfect.

No Robbie Dales, no partners, nothing. I thought 'I know what I want, with no arguments I want a crystal clear FM signal, a lot of music, all hits and everything everybody has told me they want and everything I want to do'.

And that is how *Nova* began, it was just hamburger radio, everything was immaculate. ·

There was a thing now called a super-pirate, there was the pirates of Dublin and *Sunshine* was a super-pirate, because it was always labelled and it was the one with a cash flow of about £9,000 a week and Admiral Robbie Dale strutting around.

It was a principle thing that nobody calls me bollocks if I am not and in that particular instance I had walked away clean and wasn't going to be called that.

We set the whole thing up, found good disc jockeys and the new thing was flutter three; play three records in a row, nice identification jingle, back into more great music and every record had to be immaculate, no scratches, no bangs, no anything.

We also brought on medium wave and we would not accept commercials. What I did do was go round to some agencies and said 'give me some free ones' but amazing ads

big corporate stuff and I got all those and carted them all up and we had ad breaks.

The ad breaks to me were nearly as important as the programming, they had to be dead right, in the right order, on came a jingle, on came a record, more records, more records, maybe two words from a DJ, no mention of his name or what he had for breakfast and normal DJ garbage and we did this for three months.

Then the agency started ringing up and saying 'we want to buy, this is big' so we started taking money and I suppose in five months it was number one.

The first time we researched we had 41% of the market which is unbelievable. We took *RT1* and *RT2* to beat us, next year we researched again, thinking 'let's hold on to those good figures' and we went up to 61% and this year we reckon about the same as last year, we couldn't have got any more.

The radio station has about 55 employees and the club, which is all part of it, the club props up the radio station, the radio station financed the club, so I suppose altogether about 85.

It is a growth industry which is why I think we have been allowed to get as big as we are. We don't mess with politics, we only play records, even when elections are here every station goes into this 'vote for so and so' we will not do that.

A very funny time was one of the press officers of the Fianna Fail party was on about taking ads, and I said 'I can't take ads, it's illegal' and he fell on the floor laughing, and I just won't do it.

I think we would have a very serious impact on politics so I was having nothing to do with that at all."

ABOVE: PROFESSIONALS — THE DELIGHTFUL SYBIL FENNEL
LEFT: THE GENIAL BOSS OF *NOVA*

Although still under the same laws as the mainland, the *Nova* people benefit from the unique Irish attitude to law and order — not forgetting logic . . .

"The law has been tested a bit here, where people were taken to Court. The judge asked the question 'this is a transmitter' to the Post Office engineer who was the witness and the defence stood up and said 'this could be used for other things, like an amplifier or a heater'. So the judge said thinking he was on a winner 'could this be used as a heater' and the Post Office man said 'oh yes, it has got other uses, it could warm a room up or amplify'.

'So how did you know the one you took away was not a heater'. 'Oh well it was on the air'; but 'are you sure, were these people cold' and they sold the whole thing on the fact that it was a heater. They had to give it back, went back on the air and the Post Office from then on did not want the embarrassment.

This judge was taking the piss and this particular Post Office engineer was being correct, it is not a pure science, he wanted to show how clever he was.

That is exactly what happened and from then on it was an open thing. At one point they were going to come to local radio. What people really want, not only in Ireland or England, is music radio.

We had pirates and music radio, then the British government came along and opened *Radio 1* and that was almost music radio, probably more now than it was when it was first opened, they are trying to get 24 hours a day music radio for Britain.

The unfortunate thing is there is no competition, so the listener gets bored of hearing one music station, he wants something else to kick it up the bum, give away bigger prizes, which we can do here. We give big prizes and do all the things, we break all the silly IBA rules.

I believe in the IBA framework, it does work quite well, I don't believe in the fact that you can't give away cash prizes, it is all part of the life. Needle time is silly, that doesn't exist in Ireland so we are not breaking the law there, we beat *RTE* who are doing the same but they have to programme to the whole country.

Ireland isn't all Brookside as it is here in Dublin, if you didn't hear the accent it could be Liverpool, Manchester or Sheffield. You go 30 miles from Dublin and you start to come into real old Ireland where they like the guy on the radio saying 'this is for mummy', that doesn't wash for Dublin.

What we would like to do is regenerate a daytime *Luxembourg*. We have an invisible export here which a lot of people are catching onto as not such a bad idea. Now we are not known as political dynamite or using the thing as a political weapon, we are just in it for money. We will walk straight over the Isle of Man and take in all their audience and have that all sewn up; we now are starting to make big dents in Liverpool, Manchester, all of Cumbria, the Yorkshire area round to Wales, we are popular.

It is helping local radio in Britain become what it should be, because we are giving them competition.

If allowed to continue and there is nothing more we want but to get better and that people start talking about Irish Music Radio and don't look at Ireland as some little country tucked away, but that this is where it all comes from.

Like Mexico into California, where Mexico broadcasts to California, or *Luxembourg* broadcasting to Germany and France we are doing it.

There is a free flow of information pact made with Ireland and England. There is nothing wrong with what we are doing, it is not illegal for people to listen to the BBC here. The argument also is that people have watched the BBC and listened to the BBC for 40 years in Ireland, so why can't the English listen to something that Ireland is doing. So I see it just getting better and better and just becoming a megastation.

The only buzz I get out of it now is that this is the most profitable pirate around, no pirate station ever made the money or the success of *Nova*, it is by far the biggest, with the biggest staff, no debts. If it closed tomorrow it would go out even-stevens, which is a professional thing to say.

It can be done, you can do it, buy good equipment, pay proper wages, pay all your bills and end up with a success story'."

TUNE IN

NAME	FREQUENCY	LOCATION	HOURS OF OPERATION	FORMAT
Abbey Radio	1415 kHz AM	Brandon, Suffolk	Weekdays 9-12pm Saturday 9-1.30am	Not known
Alices Restaurant	90.4mHz FM	Woodford Green, Essex	Saturday 11pm-3am	Sixties rock
Alternative Community Radio	1604kHz AM 94.2mHz FM	Basildon, Essex	Sunday Daytime	Not known
Alpha International	93.1mHz FM	London	Alt. Sunday 3pm-7pm	Not known
Andromeda Indep. Radio	103.5mHz FM	Manchester	Wed 8.30pm-10.30pm	Album rock community news
Radio Activity	93.0mHz FM	London	Sunday 3pm-6pm	Rock
Radio Alpha	90.2mHz FM	West & Cent. London	Mon & Thur 10pm-11pm	Not known
Radio Albatross	96.3mHz FM	Sussex	Sunday 7pm-9pm	Not known
Radio Amanda	1404kHz AM	Wood Green, London	Weekend afternoons	Rock/oldies
Radio Aquarius	92.5mHz FM	West Wickham, Kent	Monday 7pm-10pm	Not known
Radio Atlantis Medway	92.5mHz FM	South London	Sunday 1pm-4pm	Not known
Bookham Radio	90.9mHz FM	Surrey	Irregular	Not known
Border Radio	90.2mHz FM	Twickenham	Late night, irregular	Not known
Radio Boulogne Litoral	103.7mHz FM	Boulogne, France	(Eng) Mon 8.30pm-5am	Magazine prog
Cambridge Community Radio	96.6mHz FM	Cambridge	Currently inactive	Community prog.
Castle Radio	93.7mHz FM	Wiltshire	Sunday 7pm-10pm	Not known
Central Radio	1359kHz AM 104mHz FM	Merseyside	Saturday noon-7pm Sunday 10am-late	Pop/rock
City Sounds	92.0mHz FM	London	Monday 7pm-10pm	Soul/rock/futurist
Comsat Radio	1386kHz AM	Woodford Green, London	Sunday noon-12pm	New wave music
County Radio	94.2mHz FM 1323kHz AM	Edenbridge, Kent	Sunday 2pm on (Bank Holidays)	Top 40/Album
Radio Caroline	963kHz AM	Thames Estuary	7am-2am daily	album rock
Radio City	90.3mHz FM	Gravesend	Wed 8pm-midnight	Soft rock
Radio Contact	1612kHz AM	Croydon	Not known	Not known

NAME	FREQUENCY	LOCATION	HOURS OF OPERATION	FORMAT
Douglas Valley Community Radio	102.5mHz FM	Wigan	Sunday 7pm-12pm	Local info various music
DBC/Rebel Radio	103.8mHz FM	London	Friday 6pm-midnight	Reggae plus
Radio Ditt	90.1mHz FM 1602kHz AM	Surrey	Irregular	Not known
Eagle Radio	98.0mHz FM	Merseyside	Thursday & Sunday	Pop/rock/
Electronic Sound Transmission	94.1mHz FM	Birmingham	Sunday 11am-2pm	Rock/comedy
Epsilon	103.2mHz FM	London	Friday 9/10pm till late	Magazine prog.
Radio Earwig	1132kHz AM VHF not known	Wiltshire	Sunday 3-3.45pm	Local info
Radio Elenore	1413kHz AM	Merseyside	Sat & Sun 9am-9pm	Pop/rock
Radio Eleven	1179kHz AM	Manchester	Not known	Continuous music
Flashback Radio	92.0mHz FM 92.5mHz FM	London	Sunday 6-9pm	Jazz/Funk
Forestside Radio	90.2 mHz FM	London	Fridays	Not known
Radio Fiona	1566kHz AM 1485kHz AM	Hitchin	Not known	Rock
Radio Floss	1350kHz AM	London WC1	Sunday 10am-4pm	Heavy metal
Radio Free City	95.7mHz FM	Edinburgh	Sunday 7-10pm	Not known
Radio Free London	92.1mHz FM	London	Sunday 6pm-12pm	Not known
Radio Freedom	1242kHz AM	Derby	Sunday 3pm-midnight	Rock/heavy metal
Radio Freedom International	98.0mHz FM	Edinburgh	Sunday 9an-12am	Oldies
Radio Funky	104mHz FM (varies)	Leeds	Sunday 7-7.50pm	Not known
Radio Gamma	94.2mHz FM	London	Thursday 8pm-10pm	Not known
Horizon FM	94.4mHz FM	SE London	Wed pm, Thur 10am Sunday 8-12pm	Jazz/Funk
Home Brew Radio	90.0mHz FM	London	Sunday 7pm-10pm	Not known
Radio Infinity	192.4mHz FM	London	Friday 8pm	Soul/funk
Radio Invicta	92.4mHz FM	S. London	Sunday 9am-3am	Soul/jazz/gospel
Radio Jackie	1323kHz AM	SW London	23 hours 7 days	Commercial
Radio Jackie North	945kHz AM	Merseyside	Sat/Sun noon-8pm	Rock
JFM	94.2mHz FM 103.7mHz FM	SW London	Planned 24 hour	Jazz/funk

NAME	FREQUENCY	LOCATION	HOURS OF OPERATION	FORMAT
KFM	94.1mHz FM	Wilmslow	6 hours a day planned	Pop/rock
Radio King	1404kHz AM	Leicester	Bank holidays	Rock
Radio Lion	90.2mHz FM	Hertforshire	Sunday 7pm-10pm	Not known
Liberation Radio	92.6mHz FM	London	Tuesday 7pm-11pm	Not Known
Radio Liberty	96.3mHz FM	Sussex	Sunday 7pm-10pm	Not known
London Music Radio	94.4mHz FM	N.London	Saturday 6-12pm	Rock/comedy
London Town Radio	91mHz FM	Middlesex	Not known	Soul/jazz funk
London Weekend Radio	92.6mHz FM	Sutton	Saturday 8am-1am	Pop, Top 40
Manchester Alt. Radio	104.0mHz FM	Manchester	Saturday 7-9pm	Rock/pop
Merseyland Alt. Radio	1137kHz AM 92.5mHz FM	Merseyside	Sat/Sun daytime	Pop/rock
Merseyside Free Radio	1139kHz AM	Merseyside	Sunday 11am-7pm	Rock/Top 40
Radio Nemesis International	1359kHz AM	Merseyside	Friday 11am-8pm	Pop/rock
Radio North Staffs	97.5mHz FM	Stoke-on-Trent	Not known	Not known
Radio Nova	1305kHz AM 92.1mHz FM 97.6mHz FM	Derby	Sunday 7pm onwards	Not known
Radio Nova	88mHz FM 819kHz AM	Dublin	24hours, 7 days	Top 40, classics
Newtown Radio	90.6mHz FM	Stevenage	Wednesdays	Not known
Open Access Radio	103.8mHz FM	London	Wednesday 7pm-11pm	Not known
Our Radio	103.7mHz FM	W. London	Wednesday 5pm-12pm	Open access
Open Asylum	87.5mHz FM	Chesterfield	Irregular	Not known
Parkside Radio	89.9mHz FM	SW London	Sunday 11am-5pm	Not known
Radio Orion	90.2mHz FM	W. London	Sunday 1pm-5pm	Not known
Radio Phoenix	94.4mHz FM	Wolverhampton	Alternate Sundays	Not known
Phoenix Radio	90.4mHz FM	Essesx/NE London	Saturday 5-11pm	Rock/new wave
Rebel Radio	93.0mHz FM	London	Sunday 1pm-5pm	Not known
Radio Sovereign	1494kHz AM	Twickenham	7am-midnight daily	Oldies
Radio Spectrum	91.8mHz FM	Chertsey	Saturday 6pm-2am	Not known
Radio Suburbia	91.9mHz FM	Croydon	Saturday 7.30pm-24.00	
SCR (Storeton Community Radio)	1296kHz AM	Birkenhead	Daily, daytime	Old pop

NAME	FREQUENCY	LOCATION	HOURS OF OPERATION	FORMAT
Shropshire Sound	94.2mHz FM 1404kHz AM	Telford	Not known	Not known
Skyline Radio	11413kHz AM	S. London	24 hours, 7 days	Pop
Sounds Alternative	1179kHz AM	Birmingham	Alt. Sunday afternoons	Rock/reggae
South East Sound	1242kHz AM	SE London	Sunday noon-4pm	Rock, etc
South London Radio	92.5mHz FM	S. London	Saturday 6pm-3am	Not known
South West Radio	103.8mHz FM	S. London	Sunday 11am-3pm	Not known
Shoreline 105	105.0mHz FM	Anglesey	Just testing	Not known
Station M International	1413kHz AM	Merseyside	Sunday 11am-8pm	Rock
Radio Star	94.2mHz FM	West Midlands	Sunday from 9pm	Not known
Sunshine Radio	1017kHz AM 94.2mHz FM	Leominster, Herts	Daily 6am-8pm	Pop, own news
Sunshine Radio	98.0mHz FM	Brighton	Sunday 10am-10pm	Rock, etc
Surrey Broadcasting Service	91.9mHz FM	Chessington	Not known	Not known
Thameside Radio	90.4mHz FM	London W5	Sunday 7pm-11pm	Top 40/album
Radio Telstar	92.5mHz FM	South Norwood	Sunday 7pm-9pm	Not known
Radio Terrapin	103.0mHz FM	Tollerton, Notts	Not known	Pop
Robin Hood Radio	94.4mHz FM	Nottingham	Testing	Not known
UK Radio	94.0mHz FM	Wolverhampton	Alt. Sunday 7pm	Not known
UKGM (United Kingdom Good Music)	90.2mHz FM	Salisbury	Tuesday 7-10pm	Jazz, blues
Uptown Radio	94.4mHz FM	Chertsey	Sunday 7-9pm	Not known
Radio Veronica	1413kHz AM	Merseyside	Monday6-12pm	Unusual rock, etc
Weaver Sound Radio	1408kHz AM	Cheshire	Some Suns 10am-5pm	Pop/rock
West London Radio	92.4mHz FM	W.London	Wednesday evening	Not known
West Midland Free Radio	?mHz FM	Wolverhampton	Not known	Not known
Wrekin City Radio	94.2mHz FM	Telford	Alt. Sundays noon-2pm	Not known
Radio Xanadu	?kHz AM	W. Croydon	Sundays, irregular	Not known
Radio Zeta	96.3mHz FM	Sussex	Sunday 9pm-10pm	Not known
Radio Zodiac	94.4mHz FM	London	Sunday noon-7pm	Not known

PIRATE STATION'S ARE TRACED BY THEIR BROADCAST FREQUENCY. THESE WAVELENGTHS MAYBE OUT OF DATE THE MINUTE THE STATION LEAVES THIS RECORDED FREQUENCY. THEY ARE, HOWEVER, ACCURATE AT THE TIME OF PRINTING (NOVEMBER 1984)

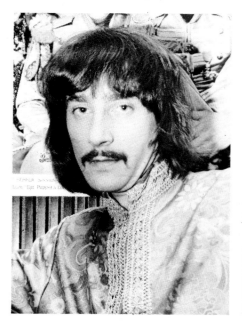

Stuart Henry born 1942 in Scotland. Actor, broadcaster and radio DJ for *Radio Scotland, Radio One* and *Radio Luxembourg.* Since developing Multiple Sclerosis, Stuart has used his creative abilities to aid research into the illness. A radio presenter noted for his appeal to all ages, he lives in the Grand Duchy and works closely with his wife, Ollie, at *Radio Luxembourg*.

Mike von Joel born 1952 in Scarborough, Yorkshire. Educated Doncaster, Winchester and London, graduating in Fine Art. Works as a publisher and newspaper editor, and lives in London and Kent.